# Rough Guide Credits

Text editors: Joe Staines, Andrew Dickson
Series editor: Mark Ellingham
Production: Helen Prior, Julia Bovis

# Publishing Information

This edition published February 2002 by Rough Guides Ltd,
62–70 Shorts Gardens, London WC2H 9AH

## Distributed by the Penguin Group

Penguin Books Ltd, 80 Strand, London WC2R ORL
Penguin Putnam, Inc., 375 Hudson Street, New York 10014, USA
Penguin Books Australia Ltd, 487 Maroondah Highway,
PO Box 257, Ringwood, Victoria 3134, Australia
Penguin Books Canada Ltd, 10 Alcorn Avenue, Toronto,
Ontario, Canada M4V 1E4
Penguin Books (NZ) Ltd, 182–190 Wairau Road, Auckland 10, New Zealand

Printed in Spain by GraphyCems

© Nicholas Tucker, 2002
384pp, includes index
A catalogue record for this book is available from the British Library.

ISBN 1-85828-788-X

# The Rough Guide to

# Children's Books

by
Nicholas Tucker

**ROUGH GUIDES**

# Contents

# Introduction

Some children love books, while others want to have as little to do with them as possible. *The Rough Guide to Children's Books 5–11* hopes to stimulate both groups: helping keen readers to discover new titles and authors, and less committed ones to find the book that suddenly makes reading seem exciting and meaningful. The titles chosen are some of the best, brightest and most enthralling currently in print. Such books are not just entertaining; in many cases they also have much to offer by way of general stimulation, as I have tried to indicate when discussing individual titles.

The books recommended have been divided into different subjects and separated according to suggested age ranges. These age ranges can never be exact, given that reading ability differs widely and some children have always enjoyed books aimed at readers older than themselves. And, of course, the same children may also enjoy dipping into books designed for younger readers. As always when reading for pleasure, individuals should feel free to please themselves. However keen an adult may be about any particular title, it is nearly always counterproductive to try to insist that children read it too, whether they want to or not.

But there is a lot to be said for continuing adult participation in stories through reading aloud to children, even when children are themselves competent readers. This usually proves deeply enjoyable for all concerned while allowing children at home valuable time with a parent. It also provides young readers with opportunities for talking about a story before, after and even while it is going on. Books have always offered children a chance to go beyond themselves and their own immediate experience, and it is only natural that they should often want to discuss favourite stories and some of the challenging ideas these might provide.

Titles have not been divided by gender, since the best books for children usually appeal to both sexes. While most authors have been restricted to only one title, there are many suggestions for further reading. Favourite books read in childhood are often remembered with great affection for the rest of an adult's life. I hope the same turns out to be true for some of the titles recommended here.

# Acknowledgements

I would like to acknowledge the continuing help I have received from my many friends in the children's book publishing world. Unfailingly positive, conscientious, generous and open-minded, it is hard to imagine a nicer group of people, and I have much enjoyed and appreciated their company over the years. I would also thank my other friends with whom I have so often discussed children's books, in particular Nina Bawden, Geraldine Brennan, Joanna Carey, Nancy Chambers, Wendy Cooling, Julia Eccleshare, Penelope Farmer, Geoff Fox, Peter Hunt, Beryl McAlhone, Elaine Moss, Iona Opie, Philippa Perry, Chris Powling, Rick Rogers, Morag Styles, Victor Watson and Anne Wood. Extra special thanks here to Kim Reynolds, always up for new ideas as well as a constant source of stimulation herself.

At Rough Guides I would like to thank Mark Ellingham whose idea the books were, as well as Andrew Dickson, Helen Prior, and particularly my editor Joe Staines who has been a pleasure to work with from first to last. I would also like to thank my partner Kay Andrews for her kind encouragement. And finally, big thanks to Tom, Billy and Joe Helm for reminding me once again, and so delightfully, what it is like to be under six years old; this book is dedicated to them with love.

# Small Readers

## 5 to 7

# Small Readers

## 5 to 7

While most children aged five will still need to be read to, two years later many of them will have started to tackle some books on their own. Stories for this age group therefore usually contain large print and extensive illustrations – both very useful for that time when young readers do decide to strike out on their own. As well as some reading ability, children in this age group now also possess a wide range of experience to draw upon, from life at home to knowledge about school, playgroup or nursery. Stories written for them can therefore be more complex than before, concentrating not just on description but also on explaining what is going on in any one tale. Some of the stereotyped characters found in earlier stories will still feature, but there will also be characters who come over as more genuine and lifelike.

It is also easier when catering for this age group for both authors and illustrators to play around with some of the storytelling or picture book conventions learned from earlier books. This is because children are now better able to appreciate the humour involved when logic and normal expectations are sometimes both turned on their heads. But behind this new sophistication there remains a strong need for young readers to be able to identify with the characters in the books they are reading. Stories where the small defeat the big or where the weak overcome the strong will remain popular, with happy endings still more or less a requirement – although some fairy tales provide the occasional exceptions.

Stories now also sometimes take on small children's common fears, with ghosts, monsters or angry wild animals making various appearances, particularly in picture books. Some children may still find such things too frightening, but others may now be able to accept this stronger material so long as it is presented to them in child-friendly ways. For once former frightening objects in books are treated with humour or affection, they usually become much less terrifying to all concerned and may even eventually turn into popular friends. This is particularly true of those stories where an initially frightening presence is then shown to be either essentially benign or else considerably less fierce than the main child characters are themselves.

It is always important to see how any book is going down with any particular child, and not to persevere with a title that seems to prove unpleasing or even upsetting. Exactly which books might have this effect can never be predicted, with quite tough stories often proving very popular and other, apparently blameless books occasionally producing strong negative reactions. While children have their own logic when it comes to reacting in this way, it is usually impossible for them to explain much of this process to others. But those books they really love are always easy to spot, simply because young readers usually want to devour them so many times over.

5 to 7

# Picture Books

This section recommends picture books whose illustrations often contain the kind of subtleties that children are now capable of spotting themselves. While written texts cannot afford to get too far ahead of a child's verbal understanding within this age range, illustrations can forge ahead in complexity, stretching and deepening children's understanding of the pictorial world contained in front of them. Frightening imagery, may still be too much for some younger readers, on the other hand it could well prove especially popular with the older children in this grouping. Many of the books recommended are extremely detailed, often revealing more to the reader each time they are read. But this is not just a matter of spotting items missed before. Repeated encounters with the same picture book can lead to young readers gradually gaining an understanding of the overall inten-

tion of each illustration, and therefore why each picture appears as it does. The best picture books can indeed be "read" by a child before there is any real mastery of the accompanying words. Going through a book with a child can sometimes speed up this process, although it may often be the child who ends pointing out some of the particularly relevant detail to the adult.

## A Dark, Dark Tale
**Ruth Brown** (author/illustrator)
Mantra (hb) Red Fox (pb)

On the surface this looks such a creepy picture book that it might seem unwise to give it to a child at the younger end of this age group. Parents must make their own minds up here, always remembering that children of the same age can have very different temperaments – one child's terrifying story can be another child's favourite. Every page in this book features darkness, cobwebs and the odd pair of glowing eyes as readers are led from an overgrown wood into a deserted Gothic house with only the same black cat on every page for company. This could all be too much for some, but for others the reaction will be quite different – particularly as the author-illustrator ends her story in an entirely jokey way. After using the minimum of words, the book finally ends in an abandoned playroom where there is a

5 to 7

dark cupboard full of old toys and a mysterious inlaid box. When the lid of that box falls open, the biggest surprise of all appears – the sight of a little mouse tucked up in bed in its own bedroom, looking extremely apprehensive.

The whole book therefore turns out to be one elaborate joke, like those scary-sounding stories that adults sometimes tell to children which suddenly end on a totally absurd note. Young readers, once in on the joke, will enjoy showing the story to others who are ignorant of what is going to happen. This is a brilliantly executed picture book, full of atmosphere and alive with details that only gradually become clear through the surrounding murk. Drawing on the clichés of old horror films, Ruth Brown offers young readers just the sort of challenge that the tougher among them may

5 to 7

8

now be ready to take on. Those others still inclined to be frightened of the dark, whether in picture books or in real life, could still get some comfort from the final message that suggests there was never anything to be scared of anyway.

## How to Live Forever
**Colin Thompson** (author/illustrator)
Red Fox (pb)

This picture book has to be seen to be believed. The setting is a library of over one thousand rooms, all of which are crammed with every book that has ever been written. But once it closes for the night it turns into an amazing book city, complete with roads, canals, windows, doors and chimneys. Peter, who lives on a shelf of cookery books all beginning with the letter "Q", hears tell of a missing book called *How to Live Forever*. His search for it takes him down innumerable stairs until he reaches a dark shelf in a long-forgotten attic. What he finds there

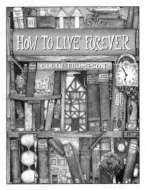

5 to 7

9

makes an enthralling climax to an unforgettable story. No child reading this book will ever look at a bookshop or library in the same way again. The surreal book city invented by Colin Thompson is utterly convincing, containing so much realistic detail that it is still possible to find something new however often the story has been read before. Literally thousands of different books are on display, each one with mock titles such as *The Lizard of Oz* or *Gone with the Wine*. These coexist with miniature trees, skeletons of birds, dolls, barges, steam trains and many other things the author-artist has dreamt up, each shelf linked to another by rambling staircases, trap doors, slides or yet more tilted books. This brilliant work shows what can happen when a writer of such talent is also a gifted illustrator.

## The Jolly Pocket Postman

**Allan Ahlberg** (author) **Janet Ahlberg** (illustrator)
Viking (hb)

A postman setting off on his bike is knocked out by a giant rattle falling from the sky. The illustrations suggest that he is living in an imaginary land of nursery rhyme and fairy-tale characters, so it's not surprising to find out that the rattle was owned by a giant baby living on top of a beanstalk. What happens next involves other well-known characters from children's literature:

first a white rabbit going down a tunnel to meet Alice
and friends; then an adventure with Dorothy on her
way to find the Wizard of Oz; and lastly, a Gingerbread
Boy goes hurtling by. But by now it is time for the
postman to regain consciousness in a hospital bed,
dreaming of all the new friends he has made.

Such, at any rate, are the bare bones of this ingenious
story. What makes it truly original is the way that so
much of the plot is told in separate letters contained in
envelopes incorporated into the
book's pages. The first envelope has
a tiny magnifying glass
hidden inside, useful for
some of the minute detail
still to come, while
succeeding envelopes continue the
story in different ways, each one containing a different
type of letter. Like some other more complex
interactive books, this one is best kept until children are
over five and when there is less risk of the messages
within the envelopes getting misplaced or lost. The text
also assumes some knowledge of nursery rhymes, fairy
tales and the most famous children's classics.

The various interesting questions this story asks also
make good discussion topics for children at the stage of
trying to make sense of everything around them. The
author wonders at one stage, for example, what would
have happened if the postman hadn't been delayed by a

11

flat tyre on his bike, thereby avoiding the falling rattle. This question is answered in a note contained in another envelope, describing how the postman marries a princess while Robin Hood gets knocked on the head instead. This introduction to the whole idea of alternative endings in fiction is yet another point of interest. Told in rhyme and incomparably illustrated, this is always a book to think about as well as to enjoy, and although it makes considerable demands on young readers it's always in the most delightful ways. One of the most stimulating children's books to appear in the 1990s, its innovative ideas have since proved highly influential though rarely bettered. The postman's adventures continue in *The Jolly Christmas Postman*.

## Jolly Roger and the Pirates of Abdul the Skinhead

Colin McNaughton (author/illustrator)

Walker Books (pb)

This riotous picture book takes place on *The Golden Behind* and features the "dirtiest, smelliest, hairiest, scariest pirates the world has ever seen." The fun that follows is fast, furious and – as in the name of the boat itself – a bit rude. Young Roger runs away to sea with a bunch of pirates who, despite their poor hygiene and a lot of boastful talk, are all really quite soft at heart.

They are certainly no match for Roger's dominating
mum who captures them and puts them to work with
all the ruthlessness that Roger knows so well.
Everything works out, however, with one more surprise
to come in a story packed with visual and verbal jokes.
This is a book that helps introduce young readers to the
whole idea of satire. By making everything the pirates
say so absurd and exaggerated, Colin McNaughton
shows children that they do not need to take everything
they read in books too seriously. Learning to
distinguish between truth and irony can often be quite
difficult for the young, which is why they dislike
sarcasm, where the words said mean something very
different from what is implied. Books like this one can
therefore be quite stimulating as well as very funny,
reminding children of the importance of being able to
read between the lines. The accompanying pictures
need no particular powers of interpretation, being as
ridiculous as it is possible to be, while the comic poems
interspersed througout the text help to make this an
absolute gem of a book. The same hopeless gang of
pirates also feature in *Captain Abdul's Pirate School*.

5 to 7

## Little Tim and the Brave Sea Captain
**Edward Ardizzone** (author/illustrator)
Scholastic (hb)

Little Tim lives by the sea and has always wanted to be a sailor. He finally decides to stow away on a visiting steamer, where he is made to work hard after being discovered once the voyage has begun. But everyone soon takes to him, and Tim has the time of his life until a terrible storm leaves him and the captain stranded alone on a sinking ship. Rescued at the last minute by the local lifeboat team, they both return to a huge welcome, with the promise of more adventures still to come.

Edward Ardizzone was one of the great British illustrators of the mid-twentieth century. In this book and its various successors prose and pictures combine perfectly. A text of under two thousand words concentrates mainly on plot details, leaving the accompanying pictures to tell the rest of the story while also describing the different characters Tim gets to meet. Black-and-white illustrations alternate with full-colour pictures, all drawn with the artist's typically lively, cross-hatched lines. Tim himself is often pictured from behind, recognizable as much by the determined curve of his shoulder as by his actual face. Older characters such as the good-humoured ship's cook also come over as distinctive individuals, again with the minimum of detail.

Ardizzone was brought up on the east coast of England, and this book, which was originally designed for his own children, contains all the romance of the best maritime adventures. The sea itself constantly appears in different hues ranging from tranquil blue to stormy green, while other pages teem with a multitude of ships ranging from humble rowing boats to loaded cargo steamers. All look somewhat dated now, as does the top-hatted reception committee that honours the brave lifeboatmen in the final pages of the story as well as the old salts who teach Tim how to make special knots and entertain him on beaches where working boats mingle with holiday-makers. Yet the story itself continues to be irresistible, combining the appeal of an impossibly exciting adventure story with a hero who never looks much more than six years old. His courage – and of course the friendship and respect of the sea captain and his crew – make for very pleasant daydream material, aided by the smell, taste and sound of the sea conjured up in Ardizzone's wonderful

5 to 7

illustrations. Few other artists have ever combined fantasy and realism so expertly.

## Ten More Tim Books

| | |
|---|---|
| Tim and Lucy go to Sea | Tim and Charlotte |
| Tim in Danger | Tim to the Rescue |
| Tim and Ginger | Tim's Friend Towser |
| Ship's Cook Ginger | Tim to the Lighthouse |
| Tim All Alone | Tim's Last Voyage |

## Mr and Mrs Pig's Evening Out

**Mary Rayner** (author/illustrator)
Macmillan (pb)

Mr and Mrs Pig are so looking forward to an evening away from their ten little piglets that they fail to notice that the babysitter sent by the agency has sharp teeth, hairy legs, a gruff voice and a suspiciously long tail. Even her name, Mrs Wolf, fails to ring any warning bells. Once the unobservant parents are safely out of the way, Mrs Wolf goes into the kitchen not to turn on the kettle but – more worryingly – to light the oven. She then grabs one little pig, but is finally foiled by a concerted attack from the rest. The story ends with the return of the parents and family harmony restored, if only just. Mary Rayner is such a wickedly funny

5 to 7

illustrator that most children will not be alarmed by
this story and any possible
implications for their own
babysitting
arrangements. Mr and
Mrs Pig look so good-
humoured dressed up in
their best clothes and
their offspring play so
happily before going to
bed that young
readers should
realize that this is a
story incapable of a
truly unhappy ending.

## Mummy Laid an Egg!
**Babette Cole** (author/illustrator)
Jonathan Cape (hb) Red Fox (pb)

Even in these unihibited times, this breezy and hilarious
picture book about the facts of life could still prove too
much for some parents to take on board. But for those
looking for an account of sexuality that tells children
what really goes on in a way that avoids any hint of
shame and guilt, this book could be just the thing. The
first half shows Mum and Dad telling their children

some of the usual lies about sex, but then their grotesque little boy and girl decide that as their parents clearly have no idea about what actually happens it is time that they were told. Drawing on knowledge presumably derived from sex lessons at school and providing their own clumsy illustrations, they proceed to tell Mum and Dad about everything as it really is. This includes intimate anatomical detail from the moment of conception – and some of the different ways adults get to this point – to the final act of birth. Books about sex for small children, although now greatly improved, still tend to be rather solemn in approach. This one is the very opposite: irreverent, anarchic and always very funny. Mum, Dad and the children are portrayed as ugly but happy, and this cheerful mood is maintained throughout. Even sperm are allowed a fish-like smirk as they race to get to an equally beaming egg ("Gotcha!"). The parent-characters in this book are still shown looking a little disconcerted at everything going on round them, and some parents reading this book might also feel rather the same way. Others will welcome such frankness – and the same might well go for children faced by a book that, at first sight, looks as if it could have been designed by someone their age. But this is to underestimate Babette Cole's superb draughtsmanship and sharp eye for detail, evident on every page of this wickedly entertaining picture book.

5 to 7

# The Stinky Cheeseman and other Fairly Stupid Tales

**Jon Scieszka** (author) **Lane Smith** (illustrator)
Puffin (pb)

This anarchic book retells familiar fairy tales as they've
never been heard before. One of the author's favourite
techniques is to give new twists to conventional endings
– so here the Ugly Duckling becomes not a beautiful
swan but an even uglier fully-grown duck. Tying
together all this amiable cynicism is the Little Red Hen
who makes intermittent entrances, beginning even
before the book has started and continuing right up to

5 to 7

the last page. Lane Smith's lunatic illustrations and a crazy selection of typefaces (ranging from the unreadably small to the gigantically large) help sustain a consistently crazy mood, very much to most children's taste during those times when they get bored with the normal run of things and long for something totally different.

But there is more to this book than good-humoured mayhem. Finishing well-known stories in unfamiliar ways teaches children something about the very nature of fiction itself, and introduces them to the idea that any tale – however well-known – always has the potential to end in a way that is totally unexpected. Author and illustrator also play around with the very idea of what a book is, turning the ISBN identification number (which all books possess) into a character in its own right. They also refuse to keep to the conventions by which stories normally open with a straightforward title page. Some critics have seen this picture book as truly revolutionary, opening up the way for even more innovation in picture books. Young readers themselves will probably enjoy it simply for its zany humour, so abundantly in evidence on every page.

5 to 7

## Weslandia

**Paul Fleischman** (author) **Kevin Hawkes** (illustrator)

Walker Books (hb & pb)

Wesley is a serious, bespectacled child living in an American suburb. His peers torment him because he is bored with their lack of imagination and never joins in any of their games. Left on his own during the long summer, he decides to set about founding his own civilization. Ploughing a patch of earth in the garden, he grows a mysterious red plant bearing wonderful fruit. These turn out to be delicious to eat, while their soft inner fibres can also be woven into a comfortable robe. When Wesley discovers he can also make a highly effective mosquito repellent from the juice, the other children stop jeering and gradually become part of his project. He also invents a new counting system as well as his own language and

5 to 7

alphabet, and when it's time to return to school, he finds he has many new friends.

This story celebrates individuality and intelligence without ever taking itself too seriously. Young readers will know that Wesley could not possibly have done any of these things, but they will still be moved by his story and enthusiastic to share in such a beguiling fantasy of wish-fulfilment. Written in a deadpan style, much of this book's impact is due to the inspired illustrations of Kevin Hawkes. He makes the huge crimson plant that forms the basis of Wesley's new civilization real enough for everyone to believe in, not to mention all the other inventions that flow from it. With children in real life under constant pressure to be the same, it is good to find a picture book so determinedly given over to one person's act of self-expression. Even though the events it describes are all part of a benign fantasy, there are valuable lessons here as well.

5 to 7

# Classics

The next section recommends classics which parents may often have read themselves when young. At a time of such rapid cultural change, it is nice for different generations to continue sharing particular favourites with each other, so giving children an opportunity to learn more about what their own parents once liked. Not every former favourite also succeeds with young readers. But other classics continue to speak to them, often with the benefit of new illustrations more in tune with junior tastes today. At their best, such classics not only entertain but also tell children something about the culture they have been born into and which they are still in the process of trying to understand. Young readers may sometimes find they feel particularly in tune with aspects of the past evident in certain classics that no longer exist today. In so doing, they will also be discovering something about

their own likes, dislikes and aspirations. Such books can even sometimes play quite a large part in helping individuals decide which way they eventually want to go later on, once they have the chance to make important choices in their own lives.

## The Adventures of Milly-Molly-Mandy
**Joyce Lankester Brisley** (author/illustrator)
Puffin Books (pb)

Milly-Molly-Mandy is an only child surrounded by a doting mother, father, uncle, aunt, grandfather and grandmother, all living together happily in the same "nice white cottage with a thatched roof". Each chapter sees our heroine setting off on a mini-adventure, often with the help of "little-friend-Susan" or Billy Blunt, a boy of the same age. No one is ever naughty or cross, and while young readers would soon get bored if all stories for their age were like this, many – little girls in particular – still have room for fantasies as universally positive as these. Rich in child-friendly language with plenty of repetition, the different stories describe exactly those things that small children have

5 to 7

always most enjoyed: going to or giving parties; attending a summer fete; visiting a cinema; setting out on a picnic; learning to ride a bike. All these things can seem particularly exciting at a young age, especially when experienced for the first few times.

Milly-Molly-Mandy first appeared in 1928, and has been entertaining small children ever since. Many of the stories now seem somewhat dated, but they are told in language that is always pleasantly direct. The unclouded vision of a past world, where everything remains forever all right, conveys more than mere historical interest. It also describes a yearning for perfection common to all humans, realized here for small children in stories written exactly at their level of immediate understanding. This Puffin collection gathers together the four separate volumes of stories (*Milly-Molly-Mandy Stories*, *More of Milly-Molly-Mandy*, *Further Doings of Milly-Molly-Mandy* and *Milly-Molly-Mandy Again*) into one book. *Milly-Molly-Mandy Stories* is also available in hardback as a Kingfisher Modern Classic.

## The BFG
**Roald Dahl** (author) **Quentin Blake** (illustrator)
Everyman (hb) Puffin (pb)

The BFG stands for the Big Friendly Giant, who suddenly and quite unexpectedly snatches a young

orphan called Sophie from her bed by moonlight. As the author himself asks of his readers, "If you can think of anything more terrifying than that happening to you in the middle of the night, then let's hear about it." But as always with Dahl, an initial frisson of fear soon gives way to rollicking good humour, signalled early on by the giant's own characteristic mangling of the English language ("Me gobbling up human beans? This I never!"). Very soon Sophie is talking to him as an equal, assisting his plans to avoid the constant bullying he suffers at the hands of other dangerous and cannibalistic giants. Later on, with the help of none other than the Queen of Great Britain, Sophie and the kindly vegetarian giant devise a scheme by which these unpleasant creatures are penned in forever.

Adults might have cause to feel anxious about particular passages in this book, for example when the

BFG discusses in juicy detail the different flavours of human flesh according to which country it comes from. The abundant humour Dahl gets from describing crude bodily functions has also displeased some, but children themselves seem to enjoy the references to "whizzpopping" most of all. Written with obvious affection throughout, the BFG's colourful and idiosyncratic language is based in part on the author's wife who was at the time slowly recovering from a massive stroke. The basic plot, in which a small child teams up with an affectionate if eccentric adult outsider, is repeated in many other stories by Dahl. Other moments, for example when the BFG goes out hunting for dreams, have a more poetic quality. *The BFG* was an instant success when it was first published and has remained a favourite ever since.

## Grimms' Fairy Tales
**Brothers Grimm** (authors) **George Cruikshank** (illustrator)
Puffin (pb)

Fairy tales were never told just with children in mind, but were shared by the whole community, which is why they often involve adult rather than child characters. The big topics they commonly take on – murderous jealousy, fierce sibling rivalry, sexual passion and parental neglect – allow even the smallest child a

glimpse of human emotions as they are in the raw. This is why children have always been fascinated by these tales, which often get closer to the secrets of their own private worlds than do many of those gentler stories aimed specifically at the young. Fairy tales also often deal with some of the great themes of all literature but in a way that is constantly accessible. Taking risks or staying put, trusting or doubting, remaining true or acting falsely, finding courage or giving way to fear – these and many other dilemmas regularly crop up in them.

There are many excellent collections of fairy tales, but those put together by the brothers Grimm have a strong claim to be the best of the lot. Classic stories like "Tom Thumb", "The Elves and the Shoemaker", "Hansel and Gretel" and "Rumpelstiltskin" are now known worldwide, and there are many other memorable tales in this book that are just as good. Although there are comparatively few actual fairies in most of these stories, an atmosphere of magic still prevails with plenty of wishes, spells and make-believe to enchant young readers. Children themselves will often just be coming out of that stage when they believe that magic is possible in real life as well as in stories. But they still often like to have fantasies about it, and in fairy tales there are many moments when the weak and the small triumph through their imaginary powers.

Children also often enjoy the strict morality operating

in so many of these stories, where good prevails and the bad suffer what can be quite savage punishments. Other fairy tales show the undeserving winning out, and this type of moral anarchy can also be popular with young children. By covering such a wide range of characters and dealing with such a variety of issues, fairy tales continue to satisfy readers everywhere. This is true whether such tales are translated from another language, as they are here, or whether they come from the same country of origin as their readers.

5 to 7

This edition is based on the translation into English that first appeared in 1823 and which was later defended by Charles Dickens when it came under attack from a school of moralists that disliked all fairy tales on principle. The line illustrations are those originally provided by the great Victorian engraver George Cruikshank. Although many other collections of the Grimms' tales illustrated by different artists now exist (and there are also legions of picture books concentrating on only one or a few of the Grimms' stories), this complete edition still has much to recommend it.

## The Iron Man

**Ted Hughes** (author) **Andrew Davidson** (illustrator)
Faber (pb)

With his great iron head shaped like a dustbin and as big as a bedroom, the Iron Man is a formidable figure who eats tractors for breakfasts and is even able to reassemble himself after falling over a cliff and breaking into small pieces. The local farmers hate him for his attacks on their machinery, and manage to trap him in a giant pit. But after climbing out he eventually makes his peace with the local community, eating away to his heart's content in a nearby scrapyard. And when a dark dragon as big as Australia threatens the whole world, it is the Iron Man, now everyone's favourite, who finally drives it away.

Subtitled "a children's story in five nights", this tale
combines a forceful poetic vision with the warm,
affectionate tones of a father telling a bedtime story to
his children. The Iron Man himself is not just a giant;
he is also the dark and potentially destructive side
buried away in all humans. When he is opposed and
denied by everybody, he is at his most dangerous. But
once people try to understand him, it becomes possible
to use his enormous strength and vitality for the good
of everyone. It takes a child in the story to realize this
after making the first overtures to the Iron Man that are
not consistently hostile. Getting on the side of the
monster rather than taking up arms against is a
recurrent theme in fairy tales, and this story could
claim to be a modern reworking of this particular
myth. It contains other elements of folklore too, as
when the Iron Man and the dragon finally engage in
one of those ritual contests of strength from which
neither side can afford to back down however dreadful
the consequences. But above everything else it is the
language of this story that makes it so memorable. This
never lets up from the moment the Iron Man first
appears on the top of a cliff to the final image of wild
blissful music made by the dragon after it has been
converted into a giant singer in space. Ted Hughes'
prose here is often close to the vivid, muscular poetry
that made him famous, and reading this tale aloud to
children will provide them not just with an exciting

**5 to 7**

31

story but also a memorable lesson in the power of words.

## My Naughty Little Sister
**Dorothy Edwards** (author) **Shirley Hughes** (illustrator)
Mammoth (pb)

Despite its title, the three-year-old sister in question is more obstinate and inquisitive than genuinely naughty. Coming up against a multitude of everyday happenings that she does not always fully understand, the little girl constantly fights for an explanation with a tenacity that everyone – author and readers alike – can only admire. Her words and actions are always so transparent that even only slightly older readers will soon realize the gap between what the little sister sometimes says and what she really means. When she is mildly ill although she refuses to see a doctor it is only a matter of time before her natural curiosity about his thermometers and stethoscopes gets the better of her. Other mini-adventures involve a wobbly tooth, a first visit to the pantomime and a traumatic meeting with Father Christmas.

These warmly affectionate and often amusing stories offer children a first inkling of psychological understanding, given that the little sister has yet to reach the stage when she is in any way able to hide her

5 to 7

immediate thoughts and emotions from others. Based on memories of the author's own sister, the girl's blatant self-interest, wilfulness and inability to understand, accompanied by an affectionate, caring nature, makes her into exactly the type of sibling an older child can both love and feel pleasantly superior to at the same time. Young readers will also remember what they were like at this age, with individual stories often sparking off memories of events

from their own past. This is a game parents can join in too, given that the plea "Tell me a story about when you were once naughty" can lead to what children often consider some great parental stories in return. Further stories can be found in *When My Naughty Little Sister Was Good*, *My Naughty Little Sister's Friends* and *My Naughty Little Sister and Bad Harry*.

## The Story of Doctor Dolittle

**Hugh Lofting** (author/illustrator)

Red Fox (pb)

Doctor Dolittle is a wonderfully kind but rather vague genius who has one great gift – the ability to talk to animals. He lives in the country town of Puddleby-on-the-Marsh with Polynesia the parrot, Dab-Dab the duck (who also acts as his housekeeper), Gub-Gub the pig and other assorted animals. Human interest is represented in the person of Tommy Stubbins, a ten-year-old cobbler's son taken on by the doctor as an assistant. Deserted by patients because his house is so full of animals, the doctor – although always short of money – still manages to travel all over the world. But he regularly gets into trouble because of his determination to do good to as many animals as possible, sometimes even ending up imprisoned for a while in the local jail. He can talk to the smallest insect for hours on end, and although often muddled over detail, he is always totally clear in his own mind when it comes to denouncing cruelty – whether inflicted on animals or by humans to each other. Without an ounce of malice himself, he has a fair claim to be one of the secular saints of children's literature.

The character first appeared in 1920 and while the stories occasionally show their age – particularly in some rather patronizing attitudes towards other

**5 to 7**

countries and races – they are redeemed by Lofting's winning blend of irony and compassion and his own charming, cartoon-like illustrations. The idea of humans living in a family of animals and sharing a common language is a very old one, and it is made all the more believable here because of the deadpan way in which the doctor's extraordinary adventures are narrated throughout. Written originally for the author's children in the form of letters sent home from the front during World War I, these stories continue to relate to young audiences intrigued by the way in which they so often blend the magical with the absurd. There is also a lot of sense in the Doctor's opinions on human stupidity and the continual need for tolerance. A musical film of his adventures was made in

5 to 7

1967, but these charming stories are still the best way to get into the real world of Dolittle.

| Four More Doctor Dolittle Books | |
| --- | --- |
| Doctor Dolittle's Zoo | Doctor Dolittle's Circus |
| Doctor Dolittle's Caravan | The Voyages of Doctor Dolittle |

## The World of Pooh

**A.A. Milne** (author) **E.H. Shepard** (illustrator)

Dutton Children's Books (hb)

This book is actually two combined: *Winnie-the-Pooh* (published in 1926), and *The House at Pooh Corner*, which appeared two years later. Not only are both key texts in the history of children's literature, they also set standards of humour and characterization that have never been bettered. Milne was at the height of his powers by the time he came to write for small children, and the spoken dialogue he creates remains as fresh as the quizzical humour which permeates the books. The little poems dotted throughout have not always aged so well, but this is a small price to pay for a book that is world-famous as well as a national treasure. Wonderfully illustrated by E.H. Shepard with line drawings that later had colour added to them, this is

5 to 7

still an indispensable book for young readers, full of beguiling fantasy that often contains gentle wisdom at the same time.

The main characters illustrate familiar human strengths and weaknesses: Pooh bear, while affectionate and good-natured, is also greedy and lazy; and Piglet remains fundamentally timid. Neither is particularly

**5 to 7**

bright, and their inability to understand even the simplest of situations is one main source of humour. But whenever they get too confused, there's always Christopher Robin (based on the author's own son), to come to the rescue. The toy-animals lead idyllic lives in the middle of a Forest, spending each day doing little more than getting up, eating, visiting each other and going to bed again – very much as small children do when playing at living in imaginary houses. Enjoying all the independence of adults but without any need to earn a living, the lives they lead mix gentle adventure with an everyday existence made continually entertaining by an author with the lightest of comic touches.

The result is a couple of books that have long been popular with all ages. While older readers appreciate their clever humour, children greatly enjoy a collection of characters who understand so much less about the ways of the world than they do themselves. There is also the attraction of a dreamlike countryside existence, where – apart from some occasional bad weather and the odd misunderstanding – no danger ever threatens and nothing unpleasant really happens. It is significant that this idyll only comes to an end when Christopher Robin finally has to go to school. Saying goodbye to Pooh in the last chapter is the equivalent to bidding farewell to the whole of infancy itself. But whatever the demands life is going to make in the future, there will always be these two books to fall back on.

5 to 7

# Animal Stories

The popularity of animal stories reflects children's natural feeling for beings who can sometimes seem very like themselves. Almost always depicted as keen to try out different adventures and with no interest in school, going to bed on time, staying tidy or any of the other rules of an ordered society, these characters make excellent imaginary friends. Small children, increasingly aware of restrictions in their own lives, can therefore still let their imaginations run riot when reacting to stories about such animals. Such stories stretch from the realistic to the fantastic. In illustrations, images also range from recognizable animals to humanized creations that speak, wear clothes and often end up looking neither animal nor human. This type of variation reflects the way that children themselves often think about animals, sometimes seeing them as utterly different and at other

39

times treating them more like human friends. Some adults have criticized stories about humanized animals for providing young readers with inaccurate perceptions. But this is a purely grown-up worry; children soon get to know the difference between a genuine and a fictional animal, enjoying both for quite different reasons.

## Aesop's Fables: The Hare and the Tortoise and Other Animal Stories

**Sally Grindley** (author) **John Bendall-Brunello** (illustrator)

Bloomsbury Children's Books (pb)

Aesop told some of the shortest as well as some of the best stories for children. Eighteen of his little masterpieces are included in this picture book, ranging from favourites like "The Town Mouse and the Country Mouse" to lesser-known titles such as "The Dog and the Shadow". Each story makes sense in itself but also contains a more general meaning that readers, and their parents, are left to work

**5 to 7**

out for themselves. But this shouldn't be too hard, given that so many phrases from this ancient collection have now worked their way into the language. "Sour grapes", "A wolf in sheep's clothing", and "Don't count your chickens before they are hatched" all turn up in this book, affectionately illustrated by John Bendall-Brunello. Even wicked wolves are made to look like comic characters, along with great, puffing bulls, cheeky dogs and the occasional humans – in one case a couple of boys wearing baseball caps and riding their bikes.

Re-creating these stories in a contemporary setting is quite appropriate, given that they remain as relevant now as they were when Aesop first told them in Greece in the sixth century BC. Thought to have been a slave and possibly disabled in some way – although nothing is certain about this legendary figure – there is no doubt that his sympathies always lay with the small and weak against the arrogance and stupidity of those who are more powerful. Sheer intelligence is often shown here as more than a match for brute strength, which is why the mouse is able to save the life of the mighty lion and the reason that the fox can outwit the much bigger goat. These fables and their jaunty illustrations are perfect for bedtime when one more story is asked for and there is only the minimum of time left in which to tell it.

5 to 7

## A Bear Called Paddington

**Michael Bond** (author)
**Peggy Fortnum** (illustrator)
HarperCollins (pb)

One day Mr and Mrs Brown
come across a small bear who
has just smuggled himself into
Britain from darkest Peru.
Naming him after the railway station
where they find him, they take him back home to their
children Judy and Jonathan. After that, Paddington –
who speaks perfect English – has a succession of
adventures trying to understand all the unexpected
things he comes across in Britain. There is a disastrous
expedition on the Underground, a traumatic visit to the
seaside and an unforgettable trip to the theatre. He has
a particular talent for falling over, telling tall stories and
generally getting into all sorts of minor trouble, and his
appetite for marmalade often makes him very sticky
into the bargain. Somewhere between a pet and a small
child, he is everyone's favourite and all the brief stories
about him have unfailingly happy endings.

The broad humour and simple writing in this book
makes it particularly suitable for children not yet ready
for more demanding literature. But while they might
laugh at Paddington's numerous mistakes plus his quite
unwarranted air of overconfidence, they may also have

5 to 7

some considerable sympathy for him as well. Not so long ago they may also have got into similar states of confusion. They too may have been quite oblivious to the effect they were creating among others, or to the possibility of looking a bit ridiculous. So laughing at Paddington in these stories can also be part of the way that children mark the fact of their own maturity in comparison with what they were like as infants. In all events, the formula hit on by the author has proved immensely popular ever since this first story was published in 1958. In the early books Michael Bond's light touch was matched by the delightful pen and ink illustrations of Peggy Fortnum. She has been succeeded in more recent books by the less sketchy but no less winning drawings of R.W. Alley. Equally successful on TV, Paddington has also been sold as a toy, usually dressed in a duffle coat, broad-brimmed hat, and over-sized gumboots.

## Some More Paddington Bear Books

| | |
|---|---|
| Paddington Helps Out | Paddington Goes |
| Paddington Abroad | to Town |
| Paddington At Large | Paddington Takes |
| Paddington Marches On | the Air |
| Paddington at Work | Paddington on Top |

## Clever Polly and the Stupid Wolf

**Catherine Storr** (author) **Marjorie-Ann Watts** (illustrator)
Puffin (pb)

The wolf in these short stories simply cannot get anything right. Each time he develops a plan to eat Polly he is comprehensively outwitted by his young adversary and so ends up with nothing. While his intentions remain thoroughly evil, as a character he soon becomes an object of derision. This book is reminiscent of *Little Red Riding-Hood* with the main roles reversed: it's the wolf who gets to be the victim, and the little girl who remains in control throughout.

Originally told by the author to her own small child, *Clever Polly and the Stupid Wolf* celebrates childhood competence in a way that is deeply satisfying to young readers as well as consistently amusing. In real life small children tend to be reprimanded when things go badly wrong but are less often praised on those other occasions when they do manage to overcome new challenges. The author, originally a psychiatrist, understands this and the value of stories that make children feel better about themselves. Polly therefore emerges as a superstar in all her books, so providing young readers with an excellent role model as well as a nice fantasy figure with whom they can identify. But by setting these tales so clearly in the land of make-believe, the author avoids giving children the impression that they can indeed cope with everything the real world may throw at them. In the world of fantasy, however, children – like adults – have always been allowed to indulge themselves, and seldom more so than here. Not only is Polly quite unafraid of the wolf, she actually worries about him too. He and Polly repeat the same situation over and over again but in ways that remain interesting and unexpected each time. Catherine Storr wrote a number of sequels to this story as well as much else for children, and her books are always strongly imaginative as well as beautifully written.

## Gobbolino the Witch's Cat

**Ursula Moray Williams** (author/illustrator)
Kingfisher (hb) Puffin (pb)

Although Gobbolino is born a witch's cat, he never gets anywhere near to fitting into the role. Instead of possessing coal-black fur and green eyes he is a tabby

45

with one white foot. He is also kind-hearted by nature, never able join in all the evil spells going on around him. Small wonder, then, that he's eventually expelled from the home of the nasty old witch who is his owner, so forcing him to seek his fortune elsewhere. But while everyone he meets likes him at first, Gobbolino is still enough of a witch's cat to get into trouble. His understanding of human speech, for example, is still something of a giveaway, not to mention his unnerving ability to make blue sparks stream from his whiskers and red ones from his nose. But eventually, after much wandering and frequent danger, Gobbolino is finally accepted as a proper kitchen cat. No longer able to perform magic tricks, he's content to spend the rest of his life peacefully by the hearth, catching the odd mouse and happily returning all the affection with which he is now surrounded.

The author, who illustrates this story with her own ink drawings, has written over sixty books for children and this is one of her best. The idea of someone small constantly in search of a safe resting place has natural attractions for children still so strongly home-based

5 to 7

themselves. The adventures Gobbolino has, which take him from scenes of opulence to conditions of extreme poverty, also have the eternal appeal of the picaresque story, where the hero is condemned to wander about the world before finally settling down. In this genre things traditionally go wrong before turning out all right in the end, so giving the story an extra depth and tension. A constant change of scenery and a stream of different characters can also be popular with young readers who often know little about life outside their own homes and are eager to find out more. Ursula Moray Wilson provides exactly this kind of interest, with each chapter so well-defined that the book can be read as a series of short stories, and readers do not necessarily have to remember everything that comes before. Long, continuous stories can still be quite taxing at this age, but no one could accuse this book of being anything less than engrossing and delightful.

## The Sam Pig Storybook
**Alison Uttley** (author) **Cecil Leslie** (illustrator)
Faber (pb)

Sam is, it often seems, a pig only in name – in every other way he's just like a mischievous little boy living with his older brother and sister in a dreamlike existence in which animals communicate exactly like humans. In

this idyllic world, there is always plenty to eat and no apparent need for anyone to work. And as for Sam himself, he is so far from suffering the normal fate of pigs that he sometimes carries home bacon rind in his pocket without ever thinking that this might look more than a little incongruous. Playing his fiddle, finding sleeping dragons, going to the theatre or attending the local flower show, he's always in the thick of things.

Told in twenty separate stories, Sam's adventures also offer glimpses of an idealized rural existence. In this world there is always something interesting or beautiful to look at, and all animals live in natural harmony with each other – even the fox in these stories is a reformed character. The author grew up on a farm and the

5 to 7

48

affection she clearly holds for her own past spills out on to Sam himself and to everything else in the countryside she describes so well – from wild flowers and berries to its background of ancient legend and long-held historical memories. Told in good, clear prose enlivened by a smattering of local dialect, these stories and their various sequels describe a sunny existence with no hint of shadow. When children want to dream about such a life, Sam Pig offers one of the best fantasy escapes ever devised for them.

## Stuart Little

**E.B. White** (author) **Garth Williams** (illustrator)
Puffin (pb)

Stuart Little is a mouse born to a family of humans. He lives in New York with his parents and older brother, and never lacks for adventure, what with the family cat Snowbell to outwit, toy boats to sail and busy streets to negotiate. But halfway through the story Stuart decides to run away in order to find Margalo, a beautiful little wren he has taken a fancy to who has unexpectedly disappeared. Although he never actually finds her, readers are given to understand that it is the search that really matters, with Stuart convinced to the very last that he is heading in the right direction.

This odd, distinctive story came to the author in a

5 to 7

dream, which he then expanded into a narrative for his nephews and nieces before finally turning it into a book. It still retains an attractive, dream-like quality, with Stuart regularly enjoying the best of both worlds – human and animal. Though child-like in some ways, he can also act with all the confident aplomb of a mature adult and there is never much doubt that he is well able to look after himself away from home. Told in a deadpan style, his adventures range from comic to dramatic, with the extra interest for young readers of seeing how a hero even smaller than themselves still manages to cope in an adult-size world. Fortunately all the grown-ups Stuart meets are kind and helpful, always ready for a chat and never in the least surprised to encounter a two-inch mouse with human speech and elegantly dressed. First published in 1945, this classic story was later made into a successful film. As a book, its episodic plot, short chapters and abundant illustrations by Garth Williams all serve to make it very agreeable to young readers.

## The Ugly Duckling: from the story by Hans Christian Andersen

**Kevin Crossley-Holland** (author) **Meilo So** (illustrator)
Gollancz (hb)

Hans Andersen was one of the great storytellers for children, but modern-day parents often dislike the excessive gloom found in some of his stories. This one, it has to be said, is a case-in-point. Before the ugly duckling finally discovers that he is really a beautiful swan, every other animal and human he meets constantly attack him simply for the crime of looking plain.

Kevin Crossley-Holland

**The Ugly Duckling**

from the story by Hans Christian Andersen

Illustrated by Meilo So

The illustrator, Meilo So, has something of a problem here, since in her pictures the fluffy little cygnet never seems at all ugly, merely a bit different. Yet this could well be the very point Andersen was trying to make, and there is no doubt that this particular story has always been one of his best-known and loved. It is not difficult to understand why: even the happiest child has moments when he or she gives way to the feelings of self-pity so memorably caught in this text and sensitively put into English by the poet and author Kevin Crossley-Holland. As for children

who are genuinely having a bad time, the promise of ultimate happiness and acceptance at the end of this tale offers hope and reassurance when in reality both may be in very short supply. Adults in later life have often said that such messages once seemed a real help to them, particularly when everything else looked bleak and sad. Andersen did not often include happy endings in his stories, but when he does – as in this case – the effect can still be inspiring as well as comforting.

## The Witch's Dog
**Frank Rodgers** (author/illustrator)
Puffin (pb)

Wilf sees no reason why a dog such as himself should not apply for the position of witch's helper – a job normally performed by a cat or toad. After many refusals he finally tries wearing a cat's mask during interviews, but this soon breaks and he's back where he started. Weenie, the young witch he has finally applied to, is going through a bad patch herself, and the two agree to join forces in the hope their luck will turn. And so it does, once Wilf fixes safety belts to the broomstick and Weenie gets some spectacles so that she can now see how to make her spells work properly. The story ends with Weenie and her faithful pet flying off into the distance for more adventures.

This book, appearing in Puffin's "Developing Readers" series, is made up of short stories that use comparatively simple words and sentences accompanied by pictures on every page. But basic English does not have to be boring, and the author-artist Frank Rodgers has a talent for producing brightly illustrated, lively stories that engage readers from the first page onwards. His pictures add plenty of detail not included in the text, such as the various grooming activities going on at the special Pet Show for Witches, or all the weird and wonderful spectacles that Weenie tries on before finding a pair that really suit her. Printed on tough paper with a special reinforced cover, this nice little book has a lot going for it and is certainly worth a try.

5 to 7

# Other Stories

Becoming engrossed in stories serves a number of needs where young readers are concerned. Stories can offer them both an escape from current realities as well as an introduction to new worlds about which they have no previous experience. The same story can also sometimes prove both amusing and frightening; happy and sad; familiar and unexpected; safely comfortable and stimulatingly different. Such stories will all be read in particular, individual ways, with each child drawing something different from the same narrative and illustrations. What all interested readers do have in common is a capacity to become engaged with stories, with particular favourites sometimes requested over and over again. This interest derives from a deep, imaginative need. No-one is as yet quite clear what function such stories actually play in child development; what is not in dispute is their evident importance to children at the time. Missing out on this sort of stimulation could be to lose sight of something of great value to a growing child, even though he or she may never be able to explain in later life what exactly this value once consisted of.

## Beaver Towers

**Nigel Hinton** (author) **Anne Sharp** (illustrator)

Puffin (hb)

Philip is swept away to a far-off island after forgetting to let go of his kite during a freak storm. On his arrival a brave robin leads him to some beavers who tell him about all the trouble caused by the wicked witch Oyin. Unless someone can stop her, every animal on the island will soon be her slave. Philip decides to invade the dungeons of Beaver Towers in order to bring back a vital book of magic. He succeeds, but not before a terrible tussle with Oyin. At one stage he has to renounce what looks like his identical twin half, who suddenly appears before him at a crucial moment.

5 to 7

Only just over 100 pages long, this story acts as a good preparation for those much longer fantasy-adventures later to be enjoyed by older children. Magic, talking animals and an atmosphere of evil all jostle together, but while the tension is at times considerable it never becomes too much. This is because a story of this length has to make its points quickly, lacking the time necessary in which to build up a greater sense of suspense and reader-involvement. The heroic Philip comes across as a thoroughly pleasing model for smaller readers who are increasingly ready now to imagine either themselves or else characters of roughly the same age caught up in equally exciting adventures far away from the safety of home. There are three excellent sequels to this story: *The Witch's Revenge, The Dangerous Journey* and *The Dark Dream.*

## Flat Stanley
**Jeff Brown** (author) **Tomi Ungerer** (illustrator)
Mammoth (pb)

Stanley is a perfectly ordinary American boy until one day he wakes up to find that he's only half-an-inch thick. He cheerfully makes the best of his new situation, easing himself under doors as a party trick and lowering himself through a grating in order to retrieve his mother's favourite ring. He also enjoys a free

holiday by getting his parents to post him in an envelope to California, and foils a robbery by posing as a picture in the local art gallery. But when other children start laughing at him, Stanley longs to be the right size again. With the help of his younger brother Arthur, he finally returns to his original shape.

Small children are fascinated by the whole idea of bodily change, probably because their own bodies and those of their friends are also in a constant process of development. Accounts of young heroes or heroines suddenly changing into giants or else shrinking to almost nothing are often extremely popular, and can be found in some of the oldest fairy tales and legends. Jeff Brown's ingenious story brings a new twist to this theme, and it has already become a classic. There is much to laugh at in this tale and something to think

5 to 7

about too. Children can easily understand why younger brother Arthur gets so jealous; they will also see why Stanley wants to make the most of his new dimensions. The whole idea of being able to do the impossible has always intrigued children, but they also enjoy being told that it's still best to be ordinary in the long run. This story has it all: the excitement of novelty and the reassurance that Stanley comes back to normality. Illustrated with line drawings by Tomi Ungerer – one of the most distinctive illustrators of his time – there is something here for everyone, including some good jokes for adult readers too.

## Follow That Bus!

**Pat Hutchins** (author) **Laurence Hutchins** (illustrator)
Red Fox (pb)

Class 6 at New End School is expecting to visit a farmhouse after a picnic in the country. But when their forgetful teacher Miss Beaver accidentally switches holdalls with a pair of bank robbers, the fun really starts. A desperate cross-country chase leads to a rather implausible farmer and his wife, who everyone but the characters in the book will immediately recognize as the two crooks in disguise. More chases follow, enlivened at one stage by an angry bull. School trips are often very popular, but they're rarely so much fun as

this. All ends happily, with Miss Beaver continuing to
mislay important articles right up to the last.

The author is also an experienced and successful
artist, though in this case her story is illustrated in great
style by her husband Laurence Hutchins. Combining
relentless action with high comedy, what children will
probably remember most is the atmosphere of constant
affection and trust between the scatty Miss Beaver and
her resourceful pupils. There are moments, indeed,
when the schoolchildren seem rather more grown-up
than their teacher, but this is a situation they never
attempt to manipulate. The feeling here instead is of a
large and boisterous family, where everyone is both
valued and happy.

**5 to 7**

## A Gift from Winklesea

**Helen Cresswell** (author) **Susan Winter** (illustrator)

Hodder (pb)

An egg-shaped stone bought by two children on a seaside outing unexpectedly hatches once, when they get home, into a beautiful, grey little creature of a type no one has ever seen before. Nick-named "the Gift", he grows quickly until he is almost too big for the Kane family's modest house and garden. Always hungry, he eventually causes trouble by raiding the neighbours' gardens. The family finally decides that he may indeed by a young Loch Ness Monster whose natural home is water. But before he is taken back to the sea, "the Gift" makes his own way there, leaving behind fond memories – plus some very relieved neighbours.

Small children commonly want everything their own way, and discovering that this is rarely possible is one of the lessons they all eventually have to learn. Stories can help here, such as this one where child characters have to let a favourite pet go for his and everyone else's own good. It's not a sad tale, since the children are convinced they will see "the Gift" again when they visit the seaside, and there is always the same shop to explore for another equally surprising present to take back home. Even so, they do have to learn that wanting to keep a pet is not necessarily the same thing as being able to retain it indefinitely, and to that extent everyone is a little wiser when the story finishes.

Helen Cresswell is a very experienced writer for children of all ages, and this story shows her skill in evoking a strange, imaginative world described in beautifully clear language. Small children are often fascinated by the various shaped and differently coloured stones they find around them; the fantasy that there might also be an animal growing inside one of them lends itself wonderfully to the sort of imaginary games they also enjoy at this age.

## It's Not My Fault!

**Bel Mooney** (author) **Margaret Chamberlain** (illustrator)

Mammoth (pb)

Although Kitty is still very much a pre-teenager, every now and again she goes through some of the sulks and

tussles with authority common at the adolescent stage. In this book, the eleventh in the series, there is also plenty to annoy her – but the real culprit is often Kitty herself. Because she sometimes says "no" when she really means "yes", she has then to put up with the consequence of actions she often immediately regrets. No wonder that Dad, Mum, big brother Dan and all her friends at school occasionally get angry with her. But although Kitty is often in the wrong she is good at finally putting things right, usually after a helpful word from a parent or a long conversation with Mr Tubs, her beloved teddy bear. Smiles all round usually follow, with Kitty now feeling as good about herself as her family and friends feel about her.

Aimed at the older section of the 5–7 age range, these short stories are written with sensitivity as well as considerable wit. Although Kitty's family is a happy

5 to 7

one, other people's contentment can still sometimes be hard for her to bear on those days when nothing seems to go right. School also comes over as a pleasant place, but an unwise word can still cause trouble, even among formerly firm friends. As Kitty treads her way through one social minefield to another, children enjoying these stories are also given the chance to eavesdrop on the internal dialogues she is conducting. They can see in particular how Kitty's anger with others often eventually turns into annoyance with herself for having caused the trouble in the first place. These elementary lessons in child psychology are made all the easier for readers to follow because Kitty is such a human character – neither demon nor paragon.

The story ends with the death of a much-loved grandmother, but parents who feel that this might prove too upsetting for their own children could still sample some of the other stories about Kitty and her family. While the main topic in this book is the difficulty children – as well as everyone else – sometimes have about apologizing even when they are clearly in the wrong, other subjects taken up in different titles include the problems that can arise when feeling bored, scared or simply in one of those moods when everything seems thoroughly unfair. Brightly illustrated by Margaret Chamberlain, these stories are wise as well as perceptive.

5 to 7

## The Littlest Dragon

**Margaret Ryan** (author) **Jamie Smith** (illustrator)

Collins (pb)

It is not easy being the littlest dragon in a family of ten, but these two stories show how intelligence can always compensate for size. In the first tale, the littlest dragon has to find a way of getting his share of the giant bed where he and his nine older brothers all sleep. In the second, he discovers how to make his previously unwilling siblings share their football clothes with him.

Abundantly illustrated by Jamie Smith, these dragons are Dr Seuss-type grotesques covered in scales and with tails to match. But under this disguise they are essentially human children in a very human situation. Descriptions of fierce sibling rivalry have always had their place in fairy tales and legends, and this is a theme all children with brothers or sisters of their own can readily identify with. But it is treated here with such good humour, both in text and illustrations, that any negative feelings stirred up by the story will soon be driven out by laughter. Even so, children may still feel a surge of pleasure as the smallest and weakest dragon gets his way in the end. He stands not just for the youngest child in the family but also for all small children in a world that must so often seem to them designed only with the interests of the big and powerful in mind. Written for the younger section of this age group, this is an ideal story for children just starting to read by themselves. Just as enjoyable are *The Littlest Dragon Gets the Giggles* and *The Littlest Dragon at School*.

## Matilda
**Roald Dahl** (author) **Quentin Blake** (illustrator)
Jonathan Cape (hb) Puffin (pb)

In this famous story a sensitive and clever little girl is lumbered with nasty parents and a terrible

headmistress. In real life this would be hard to bear, but Dahl's gift for humour (allied to Quentin Blake's witty cartoon-like drawings) has made this one of the most popular stories ever written for children. Like Cinderella, Matilda gets the right sort of help just when she needs it most – nothing less, in fact, than the ability to make things happen simply by the power of thought.

But although this magical gift works wonders, Matilda is shown to be almost as resourceful without it. Despite being only five years old, she can read whatever is put down in front of her, outwit any adult standing in her way and perform brilliantly at every lesson at school. She is also affectionate, modest and popular with everyone except for the villains in her life, who unfortunately include her own father and mother.

Unruly, unpredictable, opinionated and often completely over-the-top, this story offers children the pleasure of seeing various rules of good behaviour uproariously broken by the author himself. Rude about people he detests, outspoken in his views about modern developments he dislikes, Dahl holds forth in this book without inhibition. But because his is so funny at the same time, children soon realize that such aggression is not really meant to be taken too seriously. He is constantly on the side of those who are kind, intelligent and want to do the best for everyone, particularly when such people are small children like Matilda herself.  By contrast, he invests his various villains with impossibly bad habits expressed in language so exaggerated that laughter is the only response. Miss Trunchbull, the wicked headmistress of Matilda's school, is so entertainingly awful that children long for her presence on these pages even when she is behaving at her worst.

Beneath all the knockabout humour there's also a story of wish-fulfilment at its most satisfying, when

5 to 7

unappreciative parents and tyrannous head teachers, are rendered both ridiculous and eventually helpless, all through the efforts of a small child. By the end of her story Matilda has left home in order to live with Miss Honey, her aptly named form teacher. The idea of abandoning negligent parents is understandably not something taken lightly by children, but in Dahl's world anything is made possible. He also has a knack for keeping a story going while talking directly to children about whatever subject takes his fancy. This story is one of his very best, displaying just the type of verbal fireworks that have encouraged children to choose him so consistently as their favourite author.

## Mr Majeika

**Humphrey Carpenter** (author) **Frank Rodgers** (illustrator)
Puffin (pb)

The children of Class Three know they are in for some surprises when their new teacher Mr Majeika flies into the classroom on a magic carpet. Middle-aged, bright-eyed and with a pointed beard, he tells his pupils that although he is a wizard he is now trying his best to be a thoroughly ordinary teacher. But bad boy Hamish Bigmore proves such a nuisance that despite his good intentions Mr Majeika one day inadvertently turns him into a toad. Disaster is avoided only when the former

wizard finally remembers how to restore Hamish back to his old shape, but there are still plenty of adventures to come before the end of term, with the promise of many more in succeeding stories.

This book is aimed at what the publishers describe as confident readers, defined here as those who can manage longer and more developed stories. But there are plenty of pictures as well, provided by the excellent Frank Rodgers. Happy stories about a thoroughly nice school, like the

one described so affectionately in this book, do more than merely entertain. They also help spread the idea that schools can be friendly places, especially for smaller children. Young readers, some of whom may not yet have started full-time education themselves, are thereby given something to look forward to rather than dread.

The author – who has also written extensively about children's literature – acknowledges the help he received from schoolchildren when writing this story, and there is indeed much to amuse all young readers here, from moments of slapstick to occasions when the whole class has to puzzle out the best thing to do. Wizards can sometimes be quite menacing characters for this age, especially when they are wicked as well. But mild-mannered Mr Majeika simply isn't capable of frightening anyone, even if he wanted to. Undemanding, well-written and full of easy humour, this is the sort of book young readers could well try for themselves, perhaps after having heard it read aloud first.

## More of Mr Majeika

Mr Majeika on
   the Internet
Mr Majeika and
   the Haunted Hotel
Mr Majeika's Postbag
Mr Majeika and
   the School Play

Mr Majeika and
   the Dinner Lady
Mr Majeika and
   the Ghost Train
Mr Majeika and
   the Music Teacher
Mr Majeika Vanishes

**5 to 7**

## Ms Wiz – Millionaire

**Terence Blacker** (author)

**Tony Ross** (illustrator)

Macmillan (hb)

Ms Wiz is a private paranormal detective who travels around in a black van with the words *Wizard Security Agency* printed on its side in gold letters. She employs a number of gadgets, including a small, white plastic card with the power to reveal the criminal she is after. But despite a series of astonishing burglaries at the local school – including three video cameras brought in by the local policeman and then stolen from under his nose – the authorities decline all Ms Wiz's offers of help. But since she knows who has committed these crimes anyway, she goes to have the matter out with the notorious Lightly family in their own home. Once there, she inadvertently shows "Dodgy Dave" Lightly how to read the future, with the result that he's now able to win next Saturday's lottery. But as Ms Wiz's magic can never be used for personal gain, she now finds that she has lost all her powers.

The way in which she manages to retrieve the situation takes up the rest of this cheerful, easy-to-read book, which is one of many about the same intrepid young woman. Previous adventures include a

**5 to 7**

mathematical barn owl, a magic rat and an adventure involving rescuing a friend from becoming a zombie slave in the underworld. The author writes with an admirably light touch and in Ms Wiz he has created a role model where (for once) it's a powerful young female who goes on to enjoy all the various adventures. Illustrated by Tony Ross in scratchy black-and-white drawings, the whole atmosphere is one of great fun for all concerned – including of course young readers themselves.

### More of Ms Wiz

Ms Wiz Smells a Rat
Ms Wiz Banned
Ms Wiz Spells Trouble
Ms Wiz Goes
  to Hollywood

Ms Wiz and the
  Sister of Doom
Ms Wiz Supermodel
Ms Wiz Goes Live
Ms Wiz Loves Dracula

## The Romantic Giant
**Kaye Umansky** (author) **Doffy Weir** (illustrator)
Puffin (pb)

Waldo the giant has fallen heavily in love with fair-haired, blue-eyed Princess Clarissa after seeing her picture in a magazine. He tells his neighbouring

giantess Heavy Hetty about his passion, and picks up some grudging tips from her on what he should do next. Poems, chocolates and flowers all fail to work, but even these are more successful than Waldo's final attempt at serenading Clarissa with a performance of "Ten green bottles", the only song he knows from start to finish. Told to clear off by an angry royal court, he returns to Hetty with a suggestion for a bit of arm-wrestling by moonlight. She blushes and accepts.

This short, easy-to-read story is complemented throughout by Doffy Weir's extremely funny illustrations. When Waldo pledges to provide Princess Clarissa with a proper kitchen, he is shown holding up a glossy magazine entitled "Ideal Caves". Hetty herself, with her lurid nail varnish, punk haircut and bulging wrestler's figure, is also a joy to look at, and young readers will guess

long before Waldo that she is actually quite jealous of
the beautiful princess currently claiming so much of his
attention. Accompanying pictures of diminutive sheep
in the background remind readers that these are still
giants, if only in size. But in every other way Waldo and
Hetty are amiable figures of fun, far removed from the
frightening figures of fairy tale and legend that might
have troubled readers when they were younger.
Transforming former monsters into regonizable human
types is a characteristic of modern children's literature,
with this funny, endearing story providing an excellent
example of how this can be done successfully.

## Sea-Cat and Dragon King

**Angela Carter** (author) **Eva Tatcheva** (illustrator)
Bloomsbury (hb & pb)

Sea-Cat lives on the bottom of the ocean, along with
assorted sea-lions, sea-horses and sea-urchins. He and
his mother eat sea-cucumbers, chase away sea-slugs
from their garden and gaze up at the starfish at night.
Because sea-cat's fur would get matted and soggy in the
water, his mother knits him a beautiful suit
embroidered with shells, bits of bottle glass and pieces
of tin plate gathered from shipwrecks. News of this suit
reaches Dragon King, the painfully plain Lord of the
Ocean. He kidnaps Sea-Cat in order to get the suit that

might cure his ugliness, but is soon persuaded that it would be better if he had one made to measure instead. Sea-Cat's mother duly obliges, and is made a sea-duchess in return as Dragon King finally comes into his own. When he makes a heroic entrance in his new finery, all the creatures of the ocean bottom clap their finny hands together in applause.

**5 to 7**

This is the only children's book written by Angela Carter, although she translated and collected a number of fairy and folk tales, and it has some of the genius of legend itself, with its combination of strangeness and logic. Fairy tales have often described kingdoms at the bottom of the sea, and this story will soon persuade young readers that such a life can at least be imagined. Sea-Cat's actual house, made of pink and white coral with curtains of fishing nets, has a poetic quality that makes it particularly memorable. The story of ugliness cured by kindness is not new but it is told well, and Eva Tatcheva's line illustrations have a watery magic of their own. Not all novelists who write primarily for adults have succeeded when addressing children, but Angela Carter would surely have written many other excellent children's books had she not died so prematurely.

## Sophie's Lucky
**Dick King-Smith** (author) **David Parkins** (illustrator)
Walker (hb & pb)

This is the last of six stories about an engaging seven-year-old called Sophie who lives in the countryside and wants one day to be a lady farmer. Although the tone is realistic throughout, the atmosphere is one of sustained happiness: Sophie adores all her pets, loves her parents and has a particularly soft spot for her aged great-aunt Al. She chats each day with her two brothers, her parents and whoever else will listen, including her boyfriend Andrew, whom she has decided to marry when they both get to their eighteenth birthdays. A wonderful holiday with Great-Aunt Al up in the Scottish highlands is followed by a major surprise,

5 to 7

where everything Sophie has ever wanted suddenly and unexpectedly becomes possible after all.

Meticulously illustrated by David Parkins with plenty of finely drawn detail, these stories mix truth and fantasy in equal measure and with consistent charm. In

the first chapter, Sophie commiserates with her black cat Tomboy for the fact that this pet is now spayed and can therefore have no more kittens. The matter-of-fact way in which this one-sided dialogue takes place is typical of the author's approach, where young readers are given accurate information about the realities of living in the country. When Sophie sets out to groom a neighbouring pony, the amount of detail that follows makes it clear that there is going to be plenty of work here before the job is finished. When Great-Aunt Al suddenly dies in her sleep at the age of 83, the children are told the next day. The fact that she had a good life

and an untroubled death is accepted by everyone in this story, both child and adult, as reason not to feel too sad. When it transpires that Al has left the family all her money and her beautiful farm to Sophie herself, the tone is one of celebration mingled with a sense that life goes on. Sophie finally gets the pony she has always dreamed of, and on that happy note the story (and indeed the whole series) ends. The author is an immensely skilled writer for children, never talking down to them but always easily comprehensible as well as constantly in touch with their most precious dreams and desires. There are five other books in the series: *Sophie's Snail*, *Sophie's Tom*, *Sophie Hits Six*, *Sophie in the Saddle* and *Sophie is Seven*.

## The Warrior and the Moon

**Nick Would** (author) **Evie Safarewicz** (illustrator)
Frances Lincoln (hb & pb)

The five original stories in this book were created around the beliefs of the Maasai, a nomadic African tribe who live in Kenya and Tanzania. Famed for their bravery and physical grace, they have kept up close links with the natural world around them despite the growing difficulties facing any nomadic population in an increasingly regulated world. Intrigued by these dignified, proud and unique people, the author made

many visits to Maasai territory. Staying up through the African night round a camp fire and listening to their chants and stories proved an unforgettable experience. This book is one result, drawing on Maasai names, geography and myths while the illustrator, Evie Safarewicz, re-creates in glowing colours one of the most beautiful – and still semi-deserted – parts of Africa.

The stories themselves range from the exploits of brave young people, male and female, to tales of what happens when the Leopard God, who is also the God of Rain, has been absent for over eight years. The final story, "Footprints in the Wind", describes some of the ways in which junior Maasai warriors are initiated into manhood, a process that involves going through a number of well-defined rituals. This could hardly be a more different world than the one most British readers are accustomed to, but it is made to seem all the more attractive here because of its great qualities. Courage in the face of danger and compassion towards others, human or animal, when they are truly in need are two important tenets in the Maasai philosophy. The stories here featuring these and other virtues are genuinely eye-opening, painting a picture of a world that might slowly be disappearing but which still has much to teach the rest of us.

5 to 7

# The Worst Witch
**Jill Murphy** (author/illustrator)
Puffin (pb)

Mildred would be very happy at Miss Cackle's Academy for Witches – if only she could stop doing everything wrong. Whether she's forgetting spells, having trouble with her broomstick or putting her hat on back to front, everything serves to irritate her strict classroom teacher Miss Hardbroom almost beyond endurance. Finally Mildred decides to run away, only to discover a plot in progress just outside the school grounds to seize the building and then turn pupils and teachers into frogs.

Revealing all on her swift return, Mildred – popular at last – also manages to win everyone's respect as well.

Written in 1974, this book and its various sequels anticipate the type of detail that has made J.K.

Rowling's more recent Harry Potter stories so popular. Many of the main ingredients of each story are also very similar, including a classroom teacher who is particularly tough on Mildred and her best friend Maud but also a kindly headmistress who always has their best interests at heart. There is also a sneaky girl rival who tries to make Mildred's life even more difficult, and detailed descriptions of various lessons in applied witchcraft and potions. But while Rowling's books also contain an air of menace, the atmosphere here is altogether much lighter. The author always writes amusingly, and her numerous illustrations – often in black silhouette – make it clear that nothing is ever to be taken too seriously. Behind all the laughter there is also the pleasing fantasy in these pages of otherwise ordinary children who suddenly possess supernatural magical powers, even though in Mildred's case these rarely work out as she has intended. Infant girls in school playgrounds often vie with each other to play the part of the wicked witch in their imaginary games, enjoying the sensation of power as fellow pupils try to get away from them as quickly as possible. There is no wickedness to speak of in these stories, but plenty of moments where child readers can share once again in the particular fantasy of holding sway over their contemporaries. Other titles in the series include *The Worst Witch Strikes Again*, *A Bad Spell for the Worst Witch* and *The Worst Witch All at Sea*.

# Poetry

At an early stage of development, the sounds of words can be as important to children as their meanings, with particular pleasure gained from devices like alliteration, where whole strings of words are fired off all beginning with the same letter. As children get older some of their former almost physical enjoyment of poetry may be replaced by a greater interest in what a particular poem is actually about. Reading poems to children often takes second place to reading aloud the longer stories that many younger children enjoy as part of their daily ritual before going to bed. But poems can and should be squeezed in during odd moments, particularly as many of them are so short. A good, engaging poem, regularly recited (to the extent that everyone finally gets to know at least some of its best lines) can become a treasured memory of childhood itself. So too can some

of those poems that children may later go on to read to themselves or else listen to on audiotapes. Alone and with no other distractions, children can often find themselves marvelling at the sheer beauty of a poem's phrases.

## The Bed Book

**Sylvia Plath** (author) **Quentin Blake** (illustrator)
Faber (pb)

Unpublished in the author's own lifetime, this little book finally appeared in 1976 and has been in print ever since. Beds are a naturally important part of small children's lives, whether their own or those belonging to their parents, and this book invents all sorts of impossible fantasy beds, with one ingenious idea immediately capped by another even more bizarre notion. The illustrations by Quentin Blake maintain this fantasy with all his usual high spirits and visual inventiveness.

Although it's only about forty pages long and takes a comparatively short time to read, this book is still rich in ideas and bursting with excellent humour. It starts by declaring the type of bed it will *not* be discussing: "Not just a white little / Tucked-in-tight little / Nighty-night little / Turn-out-the-light little / Bed." Instead the reader is more likely to find "A Jet-Propelled Bed / For visiting Mars / With mosquito nets / For the shooting stars". Other fantasies also tumble onto the page: a Snack Bed, with a pillow of bread; a Tank Bed, with levers to pull if you are stuck in bogs; and a Pocket-size Bed, which shrinks to the size of a pea if it's not watered properly. By the time this book is finished it seems impossible that small readers will not already have started imagining the impossible about their own beds as well, and though it was described on first publication as a "good family joke", the collection is in fact much more than this. It shows children how it is possible to turn any object, however mundane, into something wonderful and exotic simply by the power of the imagination.

5 to 7

## Blackbird Has Spoken: Selected Poems for Children

**Eleanor Farjeon** (author) **Anne Harvey** (editor)

Macmillan (hb & pb)

This poet, now best-known for her hymn "Morning has

broken" (from which the title of this book comes), was for some time a leading figure in children's literature. Having enjoyed an intensely bookish childhood she always wanted to be a writer, and some of her best poems draw upon her memories of being young. Her poems "Light the Lamps Up, Lamplighter" and "Do You Know the Muffin Man?" recall the figures she heard or saw as a child, while "Bedtime" repeats those objections children still make when they want to stay up for a few minutes more. Although she died in 1965, her poems still speak to young readers today. They are mostly short, almost always rhyme and are written with clear rhythms that practically bounce off the page.

This selection by Anne Harvey divides the poems into a number of different categories. One concentrates on memories of those famous fairy stories where "Little girls in scarlet hoods / Talked with wolves and things in woods", while another section is mostly about animals.

5 to 7

A third category includes a number of jaunty history poems, such as the verse about Henry VIII that begins: "Bluff King Hal was full of beans; / He married half a dozen queens." This talent for comic writing was shared by two of the poet's brothers, who wrote a number of popular shows for the theatre in which Eleanor sometimes collaborated. But there are also poems here that leave humour far behind, describing instead childhood in all its diversity and particularly the fabulous land of the imagination to which she herself always had such ready access.

## Cautionary Verses
**Hilaire Belloc** (author) **B.T.B.** & **Quentin Blake** (illustrators)
Red Fox (pb)

These quirky poems, originally intended for a worldly-wise adult market, have also entertained children ever since they were first published nearly a century ago. Written as an acerbic antidote to sentimental or would-be improving poetry for children, their black humour and apparent loathing of young people still come over as a surprise for child readers expecting something rather different. Had Belloc really hated children the effect might have been genuinely unpleasant, but the tone throughout this volume is one of mock-severity, rather like those games where otherwise benign adults

pretend for a short while to be thoroughly nasty.
In these pages, therefore, happy endings are thin on the ground: Jim gets eaten by a lion, Henry King dies from his habit of chewing little bits of string and Matilda, who told such dreadful lies, gets burned to death because no one would finally believe anything she said. Also within this volume are the same author's New Cautionary Tales, his Bad Child's Book of Beasts and its sequel, his Moral Alphabet and a series of short poems about imaginary Peers of the Realm. Some of the more obscure references will now be lost on most readers – child and adult – but this does not really matter because Belloc knew that the sheer sound of a particular word or phrase can often please the ear simply on its own. The solid rhymes and regular metres of his poems set out to be instantly accessible establishing an easy rhythm especially popular with children. The original comic illustrations by B.T.B., otherwise known as Lord

5 to 7

86

Basil Blackwood (a particular friend of the author), are accompanied in this volume by additional line drawings from Quentin Blake. Comparisons between the two are particularly interesting, since both manage to be extremely funny but in quite different ways. The final effect is of a book that remains consistently readable, however outrageous on occasions, from a writer now chiefly remembered for this collection of exceedingly odd but always entertaining verses.

## A Child's Garden of Verse
**Robert Louis Stevenson** (author)
**Brian Wildsmith** (illustrator)
Puffin (pb)

Constantly in print since its publication in 1885, this superb collection of poetry celebrates children as major poets of the imagination in their own right. Individual poems describe the way that a counterpane, or bedspread, can be transformed by the child of the book into a land for toy soldiers, trees and houses. His bed, meanwhile, is converted by him into a boat to be steered through the night before returning at dawn to the safety of the bedroom. Ordinary stairs can also change into a ship with the aid of a couple of chairs, some pillows, two pails of water and a snack before "We sailed along for days and days, / And had the very best

5 to 7

of plays". Real things and events outside the house are seen to be full of excitement too, including railway journeys "Faster than fairies, faster than witches". A turn on a swing meanwhile enables the child to travel "up in the air and over the wall" until he can see "rivers and trees and cattle and all / Over the countryside." Many illustrated versions of this collection exist; this one by Brian Wildsmith positively glows with colour, and should prove especially popular with young readers.

Stevenson spent long periods ill in bed as a child, but these poems avoid mentioning his more melancholy recollections in favour of memories from the golden world of his imagination. These are not all benign, however, and there are occasional moments of darkness as in the poem "Shadow March" which vividly recalls nighttime terrors with "All the wicked shadows coming, tramp, tramp, tramp, / With the black night overhead". But on the whole this book offers an affectionate portrait of the child as dreamer and also as reader, with "Picture-Books in Winter" describing the joys of all the "pretty things" to be found in the pages of books, especially on those winter mornings when everything outside is cold and gloomy. Not all children were or are as vividly imaginative as the child Stevenson describes, but many will feel at home here relishing the ideas Stevenson suggests for making everyday life seem that bit more interesting.

# The Complete Nonsense of Edward Lear

**Holbrook Jackson** (editor)

Faber (pb)

One of the most important writers in the history of
children's literature, Lear stumbled into poetry almost
by accident. Employed by Lord Derby to paint various
exotic animals at his Knowsley estate near Liverpool,
Lear used to amuse the children of the house by
making up limericks. These regularly mixed the absurd
with a variety of strong human emotions, including
glimpses of the poet's own occasional melancholy. But
his extraordinarily developed and creative sense of fun
is also always evident in these poems. Despite their tiny
size, they brim over with ideas, images and jokes
designed to appeal to children's curiosity as well as to
their sense of humour. Longer poems written by Lear
later on also combine the impossible with the everyday.
Skilfully rhymed and impeccably phrased, his

verse regularly celebrates the ridiculous in ways that have always fascinated small children, themselves also keenly aware of what must often seem like the eccentricities and mysteries of the adult life going on around them still as yet only half understood.

In longer poems like "The Quangle-Wangle's Hat", Lear looks forward to the sort of zany verse made so popular over a century later by Dr Suess. Other poems like "The Courtship of the Yonghy-Bonghy Bo" anticipate the kind of inventive word play Spike Milligan includes in his poetry books. But it is the limericks that find Lear at his most effective. Many of them contain a defiant feeling for the individual against an often disapproving adult society. Those child readers who have also experienced such disapproval may often find themselves feeling sympathetic here. There is also a recurrent sense of violence in some of the images used, as in "There was an old man of New York, / Who murdered himself with a fork." Children themselves often seem to enjoy such violence, either in their own games or else in favourite literature like nursery rhymes, so long as it is made safe, as here, by a protective wall of humour or fantasy.

Above all, it is the crazy images in these limericks that seem to please most, where absurd ideas are communicated with what otherwise looks like straight-faced seriousness. The old man with a beard full of birds and other limerick celebrities are funny because in part they undermine the whole idea of adult maturity and responsibility. Reading them is to pass from the ordinary world into a perpetual carnival where anything can happen – except, of course, the ordinary and mundane. It is a tribute to Lear's extraordinary imagination that children today can still find him quite as entertaining as did his first audiences over a hundred and seventy years ago.

## Funky Tales
**Vivian French** (author) **Korky Paul** (illustrator)
Hamish Hamilton (hb)
Puffin (pb)

The author has taken six well-known fairy stories and rewritten them in the style of contemporary rap. Rhyming schemes come and go, and the print size changes according to the drama or importance of what is going on. This could all be very confusing, but the total effect works given the inspired accompanying illustrations by Korky Paul. These weave in and out of the text on every page, backing up all the action and lending an extra coherence to the verse.

The opening poem, "Jack and the Beanstalk", gives a

5 to 7

good idea of the effect Vivian French sets out to achieve. Starting with a few, ordinary scene-setting lines, over the page the text explodes into something closer to a running commentary from Jack himself: "Heigh-ho, / Give a whistle, kick a pebble, / Hop here, skip there…/ Come on, Daisy! / Heigh-ho." On the next page a twisting column of single words looks like the celebrated beanstalk itself, and very soon it's time for the famous intervention from above: "What's that? / There's a rumbling, mumbling / Shaking clattering / Thumping bumping stumping– / It's a GIANT!!!" He still keeps his "Fee fi fo fum", but everything else about this story is quite differently presented. Some parents may prefer a more traditional version, but it is a mistake to think that there is only one way of telling a fairy tale – after all, different versions of old favourites have always been around ever since folklorists first collected them. It is therefore quite possible to find versions of, say, "Cinderella" or "Little Red Riding-Hood" where details of the story and sometimes even the way it ends differ from what older readers may be used to. Small children themselves will probably prefer to stay loyal to the version they heard first, but it can also be quite stimulating for them to see the various different ways in which favourite stores can appear – particularly in a picture book as lively and unconventional as this one.

# Heard it in the Playground

**Allan Ahlberg** (author) **Fritz Wegner** (illustrator)

Puffin Books (pb)

Allan Ahlberg taught in the classroom for ten years before becoming a bestselling author and poet. His first-hand knowledge of school shows in every page of this book, as does his affection for children. Swimming lessons, morning assembly, parents' evenings, fire drill and all the other events of the school year regularly crop up in these poems, as does the memory of the fatigue and occasional irritation familiar to every teacher – especially towards the end of the school day. But however difficult the pupils in these poems might sometimes be, the mood here is always one of rueful celebration for the sheer energy, inventiveness and determination with which children will question, complain and hold forth on every conceivable topic in the classroom.

Delightfully illustrated by Fritz Wegner, the tough boys and better-behaved girls that he draws in this book are as recognizable as are its beaming dinner-ladies, tatty school buildings and occasionally exhausted teachers. Ahlberg's verse itself aims to amuse rather than to enchant. A longer poem towards the end is designed to be spoken out loud by a whole class, rather than read in silence. Each poem – however short – usually has a thumping rhythm, regular rhymes and a particular talent for word play. The poet also has a keen ear for those moments of a school day that children will recognize from first-hand experience and which many adults will recall from their own memories. He also has a particular sympathy for those children who never seem to know the answer to anything. Having already sold around half a million copies since it was first published in 1989, this brilliant collection will surely pick up many more readers in the years to come and even those children who do not particularly like school should enjoy it.

## It Takes One to Know One

**Gervase Phinn** (author) **Chris Nould** (illustrator)
Puffin (pb)

Although this is the author's first collection of poetry for children, it reads as if he has been writing for them for years. Set as often as not within school, behind the excellent jokes there are often some highly pertinent observations about the relationships between parents, teachers and children. There are poems, for example, about the impossibility of getting an adult to answer a child's questions – even though the same adults elsewhere insist that it is only by asking things that children finally get to know about them.

Illustrated with drawings by Chris Nould, there is a lot to enjoy here and also plenty to think about, as in the haunting poem "Samantha-Jayne", which begins: "Nobody speaks to Samantha-Jayne, / The silent child with the fancy name, / Who comes to school with hair a mess, / And milk stains down her dirty dress, / Who wears a coat that's far too small, / And stands alone by the playground wall." The implicit plea for more

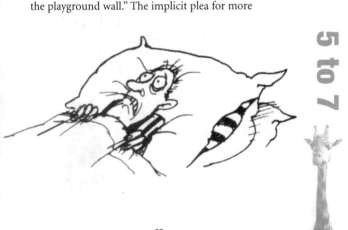

5 to 7

understanding and tolerance that follows in the last verse is well made. Other poems describe poetry lessons, reading round the class and book weeks. Reading about reading can be an intriguing idea for children, and their reactions to these particular verses could be of particular interest to their teachers. Parents in their turn could also learn something from one of the non-poems appearing here entitled "Top Twenty Things that Parents Never Say", which includes that most unlikely of parental lines, "I do hate a tidy room".

## Old Possum's Book of Practical Cats

**T.S. Eliot** (author)
**Nicholas Bentley** (illustrator)
Faber (pb)

**5 to 7**

These lighthearted poems were written by Eliot in 1939 principally to amuse his young godson, and their easy rhymes and thumping rhythms have made them popular with many other children ever since. They also display a love and knowledge of cats from an author who was always particularly fond of them,

T. S.
ELIOT
——
Old Possum's Book
of Practical Cats

owning a succession of them himself. The names he gave these pets – Pettipaws, Wiscus and George Pushdragon – are not so far removed from those of the various cats in this anthology. So while it took a child to stimulate the poet into producing these verses, the particular qualities of fantasy that went into making these literary cats such outsize and individual creations was always close to the surface of his imagination.

The best-known poem, "Macavity: The Mystery Cat" has since made its way into innumerable poetry anthologies for children. But others here are equally good, with few children able to resist "Growltiger's Last Stand", which starts in such an arresting way: "Growltiger was a Brave Cat, who travelled on a barge; / In fact he was the roughest cat that ever roamed at large. / From Gravesend up to Oxford he pursued his evil aims, / Rejoicing in his title of 'The Terror of the Thames.'" Children who love cats themselves will also recognize the truth of lines like: "The Rum Tum Tugger is a terrible bore; / When you let him in, then he wants to be out; / He's always on the wrong side of every door, / And as soon as he's home, then he'd like to get about." In 1981 Andrew Lloyd Webber devised a musical show, Cats, inspired by these poems which has been running ever since. But however long it lasts, it is unlikely to outlive the original verses on which it is based, written by one of the truly great poets of the twentieth century.

## Peacock Pie
**Walter de la Mare** (author) **Edward Ardizzone** (illustrator)
Faber (pb)

Much of the
popular poetry
written for
children today is
both amusing and
strictly contemporary in
its range of reference.
But there is also a
need for a different
type of verse
which creates
evocative rather
than comic images
in the minds of its readers. For such moods, there is
still no one better than Walter de la Mare and in
particular this collection, originally published in 1913.

Here are longtime favourites that sometimes only
have to be heard once to stay in the imagination for
ever. "Slowly, silently, now the moon / Walks the night
in her silver shoon" must surely be one of the most
descriptive poems ever written about moonlight. "Some
one came knocking /At my wee, small door" starts off
another poetic short story that has no real ending but
still satisfies because of the endless possibilities it

suggests. The poet's famous "The Listeners" is not included in this collection, but it can be found in almost any poetry anthology for children. Not every poem in this book is as romantic; de la Mare was also a skilled storyteller whether in verse or prose, and wrote equally well about more active, noisy topics such as a ship of Rio where "nine and ninety monkeys / Were all her jovial crew". But his particular gift is to catch a moment of time within which ordinary reality is suddenly made to seem mysterious and fascinating. This collection is illustrated by Edward Ardizzone, whose line drawings perfectly complement the poet's evocations of dark old houses, shadowy ruins and horsemen riding by night. The title is drawn from the penultimate poem in the book, "The Song of the Mad Prince". Only sixteen lines long, it defies any easy explanation but still enchants because of its stream of haunting images, establishing an atmosphere so immediately appealing it can simply be enjoyed for itself.

## The Pied Piper of Hamelin

**Robert Browning** (author) **André Amstutz** (illustrator)

Orchard Books (pb)

This spirited poem, excellent for reading aloud, combines high drama with a haunting story of deceit and loss. The noisy rats that afflict the little town of Hamelin can clearly be heard in the verse itself, when they drown any conversation going on around them "With shrieking / And squeaking / In fifty different / Sharps and flats". The Mayor and Corporation who try to solve the problem are as dishonest as they are incompetent, and it is hard to condemn the Pied Piper for taking his revenge when he is finally refused payment for curing the problem so successfully. But what actually happens after he leads the children away never to return? Do they really go to a joyous land "Where water gushed and fruit trees grew, / And everything was strange and new"? Or is the Piper a more ambiguous figure, promising everything but in fact leading them to a giant cave in the mountainside from which they will never return?

Different illustrated versions of this poem suggest their own conclusions. This particular edition, accompanied by pictures from André Amstutz, depicts an amiable Piper who ends up leading the children to a form of paradise. This is consistent with the general atmosphere created by this picture book, where spirits always seem high and even the rats look consistently cheerful. But the sinister side of this poem also occasionally shows itself, with the clear message that it is not always a good idea to follow someone promising so much to so many. The poem itself is based on a folk legend that some historians think may stem from the disastrous experience of the Children's Crusade in 1212. But whatever its origins, this long narrative poem by one of the great poets of the nineteenth century still manages to be as gripping and memorable as it was when first published in 1842.

## Robocat
**Adrian Henri** (author)
**Wendy Smith** (illustrator)
Bloomsbury (pb)

Adrian Henri was best-known for his work as a performance poet, and his written poetry contains the jokes, contemporary references and wordplay that have proved so popular with audiences over the years. More recently he began writing specifically for children, and this present collection gives a good idea of his whimsical, unpredictable humour. Sparingly illustrated with drawings by Wendy Smith, this slim volume, while easy to read first time, also contains much to return

5 to 7

to.

The opening verse of the title poem is a good indicator of what is to come: "Our new cat's a robot / He really is a sight / No need to feed him Whiskas / We just plug him in at night." Other poems about animals include "The Tomcat of Notre Dame", "The Lion in Derbyshire" and one of the least popular of all animals, "The Teacher's Pet". Young children will probably not understand all the references in these poems, but parents should be able to help and there is plenty elsewhere to amuse, entertain and sometimes to move as well. Readers who particularly enjoy this book could think about getting *The World's Your Lobster*, a selection of the best of Adrian Henri's verse.

## Silly Verse for Kids

**Spike Milligan** (author/illustrator)
Puffin (pb)

This book and the author's accompanying illustrations certainly live up to its name. But while adults do not on the whole encourage the idea of silliness, children usually take a more relaxed view of the topic. In Spike Milligan it could be said they have the perfect voice. Written originally either for his own children or else inspired by things he heard them say, this collection (first published between 1959 and 1963) continues to

5 to 7

be widely popular today. The author's original dedication of the book "to my bank balance" must by now seem extremely appropriate.

Beyond all the jokes Milligan is in fact a skilled poet, capable of writing verses which only have to be heard once to be remembered. One such is his famous "On the Ning Nang Nong / Where the Cows go Bong! / And the Monkeys all say Boo!" His pastiches are also hilarious, whether children recognize the original models or not – such as the touch of Kipling in "English Teeth, English Teeth! / Shining in the sun / A part of British heritage / Aye, each and every one". There are only 33 poems in this collection, some of only a few lines long, but their surreal humour can be returned to over and over again. Equally zany sequels include *A Book of Milliganimals* and *Startling Verse for*

5 to 7

# Bigger Readers

## 7 to 9

# Bigger Readers

## 7 to 9

Children between these ages who are good readers will now be able to get through most of the titles in this section for themselves. But there is still a strong case for some reading aloud sessions, if an older person can find the time. Reading aloud is never simply a matter of deciphering the words on the page. Adult narrators can also provide extra explanations as they go along as well as answering questions about the story or indeed anything else. Even when children can readily understand what is happening, they will still often want some reassurance as to exactly why things are turning out as they are, why some characters act as they do.

Part of the reason for this is that children believe that every story should ultimately make some sort of moral sense; not necessarily because they are always moral beings themselves but because they continue to expect events in the world to follow along roughly moral lines. "Not fair!" is a common accusation at this age, and it will be some time before children understand that fairness, is something that is often missing in real life. But in stories for this age, they can usually find plots where everything still works out more or less fairly.

As before, individual children will often tend to find their own meanings in stories. This may be because they feel a story reflects a part of their own lives or because it seems especially close to their own private world of daydreams and fantasies. Parents can occasionally see exactly why one book has become a favourite, but they are just as likely to be mystified by a particular book's appeal. This is no bad thing: stories have always offered a private world in which readers of any age can search for those events, messages and consolations that are especially significant to them. Such significance can often be very hard for readers to explain to themselves, let alone to others. When chatting to children about their favourite reading, it is therefore usually better to concentrate on the details of different characters or what exactly happens in the story rather than quizzing them about why they may happen to like one story so much more than another.

7 to 9

# Myths, Legends and Religious Tales

**7 to 9**

Most of the stories in this section were originally addressed to an all-age audience, and it was only during the nineteenth century that mythological and folk tales gradually became seen as more suitable for children. Since then many of these traditional stories have been cut down and generally prettified, and while this has succeeded in providing small children with some charming stories, it has also often robbed this material of much of its strength and psychological realism. In the following section children can encounter some of these classic stories in their fuller versions. Drawn from international as well as from domestic sources, these have always been close to the highs as well as to the lows of human nature. Some modern examples where authors have followed fairy or folk tale forms are also included, reminding young readers that this is a genre that continues to renew itself from one generation to another. There are also some religious stories, selected when they seem particularly close to folk and fairy tales themselves.

## The Amazing Bible Storybook

**Georgie Adams** (author) **Peter Utton** (illustrator)

Orion (hb)

The Bible (in particular the Old Testament) contains some wonderful stories, which are often neglected as a source of literature for modern children. Young readers often only hear about them – if at all – in the context of religious studies, usually as part of a debate as to whether such stories could still be seen as describing some sort of religious truth. But these stories can be enjoyed by young readers simply for themselves and their qualities of drama, insight and vivid imagination. This collection is one of many that tell Bible stories to children using simple language and bright illustrations, and with any notion of recruiting young readers to Christianity kept well in the background.

Starting with the Creation, Georgie Adams goes on to describe major biblical highlights like the plague of frogs that nearly destroyed Egypt, the mighty strength and final downfall of Samson and the story of Joshua and the Battle of Jericho. All these episodes are vividly illustrated by Peter Utton, who uses watercolours to create an effect that is consistently child-friendly. The characters he creates are more cartoon-like than real, softening some of the cruelty of the tales while bringing out their more compassionate aspects. Spies and battle plans, slavery and final escape, near-disaster and last-minute rescues – all combine here to enthrall new readers while reminding older ones quite how good these stories always were.

## English Fairy Tales
**Joseph Jacobs** (author) **Margery Gill** (illustrator)
Puffin (pb)

These tales, first published in 1890, were all taken from English sources and rewritten by the compiler in the

manner of an old nurse telling the stories to the children sitting around her. The collection contains classics like "Jack and the Beanstalk", "The Story of the Three Little Pigs" and "Dick Whittington and his Cat", but there are also a number of lesser-known tales well worth sampling. While many are also suitable for a younger age group, there are a few that parents may not think appropriate for very small children. "Mr Miacca", for example, is a story designed to frighten children off the idea of ever wandering away from home. It involves a cannibalistic ogre constantly on the lookout for small children out on their own; any he discovers are promptly popped into his bag for supper. Fortunately the hero of this story, Tommy Grimes, eventually manages to escape – but not before the sort of alarming adventures that can delight older readers as much as they can sometimes upset younger ones.

A country's fairy tales to some extent reflect its national characteristics, and the spirit of these is unquestionably one of English nineteenth-century self-sufficiency and enterprise. The occasional fatalism and strong religious atmosphere found in some European fairy tales is missing here, nor is there too much agonizing by individual characters about having done the wrong thing. Instead, if opportunity presents itself these characters will generally take it – whether they deserve their luck or whether, like Lazy Jack, they simply fall into good fortune. But underneath this pragmatism there is also a strong vein of poetic fantasy, indicated by titles like "Nix Nought Nothing" or "The Laidly Worm of Spindleston Heugh". There are also tales that are little more than home-grown versions of favourites like "Cinderella" or "Rumplestiltskin". Skilfully retold, and simply illustrated in black-and-white by Margery Gill, this is a collection that can be enjoyed over and over again.

## Fairy Tales and Fantastic Stories
**Terry Jones** (author) **Michael Foreman** (illustrator)
Pavilion (hb)

The best fairy tales do not necessarily have to be ancient; they can be written at any time, although their settings tend usually to be set somewhere in the remote past. These stories by Terry Jones revolve around the customary kings and princesses, giants and ogres,

7 to 9

witches and talking animals. But everything else about them is new and fresh, written down with the type of irreverent humour that you'd expect from a former member of the Monty Python team.

The tales that make up the first section feature among other characters and objects a sea tiger, a king who dresses like a parsnip and a monster tree with blue apples. But even this cast and scenery seem conservative compared with those found in the second section, whose heading, "Fantastic Stories", proves no exaggeration. A slow ogre who takes three days to eat his breakfast, a dinosaur who lives in a garden shed and a baby made only of snow join dozens of other unlikely but convincing creations. Fortunately the author knows that any story will eventually lose its effect if it tries to be funny too much of the time, and behind these unpredictable, zany tales there is often a sound moral point.

Other stories are so absurd there is no meaning to be found at all, as if the author wants to keep his young audience on tenterhooks right until the end. All the tales sound very much like the kind that parents sometimes tell when they let their own imaginations go wild, mixing the logical with the exotic and creating a strange fantasy world where nothing can be taken for granted. *Fairy Tales and Fantastic Stories* is handsomely illustrated by Michael Foreman with all his usual good humour and sensitivity.

## Moon Tales
**Rina Singh** (author)
**Debbie Lush** (illustrator)
Bloomsbury (hb & pb)

While there are many
collections of folk tales
for children gathered
from different countries,
this one has the excellent
idea of collecting
together stories that
feature the moon in a
central role. Tales range
from the Chinese story of "The Greedy Man" to the
Siberian "The Daughter of the Moon and the Son of
the Sun". Within these, and the eight other stories
included, the moon appears variously as a man, a
woman, a princess, a sister to the sun and, on one
occasion, as mischief-maker.

The widely different interpretations here of why
exactly the moon waxes and wanes and what causes the
markings on its surface give children a good idea of the
way that people have always sought explanations for the
natural phenomena that surround them. After reading
this collection, children may well look at the moon with
a greater curiosity and it would be interesting to then
ask them which of these stories offers the best

interpretation of what they see. They might also be prompted to write their own stories about the moon, following some of the examples in this book. In all events there is plenty to think about as well as to enjoy in this charming collection, beautifully illustrated by Debbie Lush.

## The Orchard Book of Greek Myths
**Geraldine McCaughrean** (author) **Emma Chichester Clark** (illustrator)
Orchard (hb)

**7 to 9**

As well as casting their spell over generations of artists, musicians and writers, the Greek myths have also inspired thousands of children through the centuries. Once heard, stories like "Orpheus and Eurydice", "Theseus and the Minotaur" and "Jason and the Golden Fleece" prove hard to forget, partly because their main characters display such eternal human feelings and faults. The Gods in these stories quarrel, feel jealous, act spitefully and play cruel tricks upon each other. They also like dressing up in all sorts of disguises, are up for most adventures and rarely do the safe thing when the daring option remains open. But there is another side to their lives, when a great love is won and then tragically lost, or where acts of courage are committed by heroes who seem to know no fear.

Geraldine McCaughrean is a brilliant children's author in her own right, incapable of writing a dull sentence while always staying close to a small child's powers of comprehension. Her illustrator, Emma Chichester Clark, makes her main characters look like children who are playing at what they are doing, often with the suspicion of a smile behind an otherwise serious face. In the background, temples, hills and an ever-present sea set against a constantly blue sky remind readers of the warmth and colour of Greece itself, whose three-thousand-year-old stories continue to haunt the imagination.

## Pepi and the Secret Names
**Jill Paton Walsh** (author) **Fiona French** (illustrator)
Frances Lincoln (pb)

Ancient Egyptian Prince Dhutmose asks Pepi's father, a famous artist, to decorate the tomb that has to be built before his final journey to the Land of the Dead. Pepi supplies his father with a lion, a crocodile and a deadly winged cobra as real-life models, using his knowledge of their secret names to keep them from mischief while they are posing. Much impressed, the Prince rewards Pepi with one of the royal kittens, complete with a collar made of lapis and gold.

This story was suggested to the author by her own

7 to 9

visit to Upper Egypt. Prince Dhutmose actually existed, as does the limestone sarcophagus of his favourite cat. The hieroglyphics found on temple walls are used here to inscribe the secret names of the various animals that consent to be painted, with a key for how to decipher them included at the end of the book. Fiona French adds to the air of wonder and mystery with a series of full-page illustrations, based on the stiff formality of Egyptian art. Her

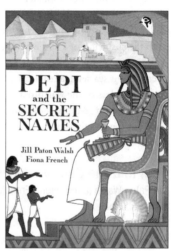

vivid use of colour makes everything look fresh and new, far removed from the faded relics of Ancient Egypt preserved in museums. By the end of the book children will not only know far more about a civilization from long ago; they will also feel that they have actually visited it. The author is a gifted writer of historical fiction for older children; this story for younger ones is equally successful.

## Robin of Sherwood

**Michael Morpurgo** (author) **Michael Foreman** (illustrator)

Pavilion (hb) Hodder (pb)

The story of Robin Hood has often been told to children, but this book gives one of the fullest fictional accounts yet of this legendary hero of the common people. It all starts when a modern-day boy dreams up the story for himself, aided by some relics he has discovered after a terrible storm. In his vision of the past he gets to see at first hand the cruel blinding of Robin's own father – the single event that caused his son to become an outlaw. More familiar adventures follow, reaching a climax in Robin's final victory over the Sheriff of Nottingham, at which point he becomes tempted by the good life in London and the offer of a position close to the king. It takes Maid Marion's

7 to 9

decision to return to Sherwood Forest alone to bring him to his senses before his final, and ultimately tragic, journey back home.

Children have always appreciated the idea of a band of outlaws, in some ways rather like the gangs they sometimes form or imagine in their fantasies. The Sheriff of Nottingham also makes a splendid villain, offending children's natural sense of justice every time he punishes a poor person who is merely trying to survive. Add a forest with plenty of trees to hide behind and branches to swing from, and you have the perfect playground for all young adventurers to imagine inhabiting themselves.

It is not often that children or their heroes are so actively encouraged to break the law of the land in fiction, but such encouragement is always on tap in these stories, represented in its purest form by the saintly figure of Maid Marion who also supplies an element of romance. Michael Morpurgo never pulls his punches as a narrator, providing villains who hiss through clenched jaws, hooves that thunder and warriors who roar. Michael Foreman, joins in the fun with full-page watercolours alternating with smaller vignettes that skillfully pick out the most dramatic moments.

7 to 9

# Seasons of Splendour:
# Tales, Myths and Legends of India

**Madhur Jaffrey** (author) **Michael Foreman** (illustrator)

Pavilion (hb & pb)

This book offers a feast for the imagination as well as
the eyes. Drawn from Hindu religious epics and other
ancient sources, stories range from how the monkey
god Hanuman helped defeat the Demon King Raaman
to the birth of Krishna and his final victory over the
wicked King Kans. There's a rich cast of characters,
including Ganesh, the elephant-headed God of
Wisdom, brave warriors on horseback, serpent kings,
blue gods, demon nurses and many others.

The best thing about this enchanting collection is the
engaging way in which Madhur Jaffrey retells these
tales; describing her early memories of how they were
told to her by various aunts or grandmothers as she
and her cousins and siblings lay sprawled together on
the Prayer Room carpet or draped around the sofa. She
also remembers appreciating the clear moral tone
evident in virtually all of these tales. Death itself is
frequently mentioned, nearly always in a far more
matter of fact way than is usually the case in stories for
children.

The author recalls how, after hearing these stories, she
and the other children would often re-enact them for
themselves, and it would be surprising if a new

7 to 9

generation of readers failed to do the same, so compelling are the characters and their adventures. A pronunciation guide is included at the end of the book for those who want to get every proper name right, and there are other moments in the text when the author introduces other details of what was obviously an extremely happy childhood. The atmosphere of contentment that she remembers so clearly comes through both in the text – where even the potentially horrific is made to seem manageable – and in Michael Foreman's illustrations, with colours as brilliant as any found in a sari shop.

## The Selfish Giant: from the story by Oscar Wilde

**Fiona Waters** (author) **Fabian Negrin** (illustrator)
Bloomsbury (hb & pb)

A giant objects to children playing in his garden, but when he shuts them out winter weather sets in and never lifts until he finally lets them back in again. A small boy visiting the garden catches the now reformed – and child-friendly – giant's attention, but he disappears and is only seen on one further occasion. This takes place when the giant, now old and grey, finds the little boy again in his garden, wounded in his hands and feet. He is, in fact, the child Jesus, come to take the giant away with him to Paradise. When the other children come to play in the garden next day, they find the giant lying there dead but still bearing a contented smile.

Christian imagery plays only a small part in this classic tale. Its central theme, which links human

selfishness to coldness and generosity to warmth and growth, is ancient, and should be readily understood by children already used to seeing different states of weather personalized in their picture books. But this

is not another story about a smiling sun or an angry wind; by taking on the idea of death, the story enters into territory still rare in picture books for the young. Parents must decide for themselves when they think it best to start discussing this topic with their children, but the final image of the giant, at peace and covered in white blossom, could offer a suitable starting point.

## The Wanderings of Odysseus

**Rosemary Sutcliff** (author) **Alan Lee** (illustrator)

Frances Lincoln (hb & pb)

**7 to 9**

Many authors have tried rewriting the story of the *Odyssey* for children, but this very full version is one of the most successful. The author, famous for her historical fiction for children, captures the

sweep of these great stories without ever losing momentum. The illustrations by Alan Lee are also in epic mode: maidens are beautiful, monsters are horrific and battles are waged with great ferocity. A sequel to the same team's *Black Ships Against Troy*, the story starts when the Greek warrior Odysseus attempts to return home following the defeat of the Trojans. He is soon beset by dangers, from the terrible one-eyed

Cyclops to the temptations of the beautiful Sirens. All the time the Gods intervene both for and against him, and there is the constant worry that his faithful wife Penelope, waiting patiently at home, might give him up for lost and take another husband.

Many of the best adventure stories describe a perilous journey, but this is one of the greatest and most awe-inspiring in the genre. Although he is brave, Odysseus is not above temptation, and part of his ordeal involves the struggle taking place within himself. His journey is symbolic of an individual's path through life, buffeted by events from time to time but in this case armed with a determination to reach a final goal come what may. This does not make Odysseus an easy character, but his courage sets an example that is still relevant in a modern world otherwise far removed from the magic and monsters of Ancient Greece.

7 to 9

# Classics

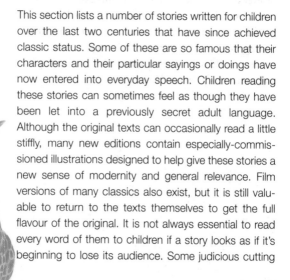

This section lists a number of stories written for children over the last two centuries that have since achieved classic status. Some of these are so famous that their characters and their particular sayings or doings have now entered into everyday speech. Children reading these stories can sometimes feel as though they have been let into a previously secret adult language. Although the original texts can occasionally read a little stiffly, many new editions contain especially-commissioned illustrations designed to help give these stories a new sense of modernity and general relevance. Film versions of many classics also exist, but it is still valuable to return to the texts themselves to get the full flavour of the original. It is not always essential to read every word of them to children if a story looks as if it's beginning to lose its audience. Some judicious cutting and skipping has always been in order when telling or reading stories to the young, and many classics now also exist in cut-down versions especially aimed at different age groups.

## Alice's Adventures in Wonderland

**Lewis Carroll** (author) **John Tenniel** (illustrator)
Macmillan (hb); Puffin (pb)

The most revolutionary story ever written for children, Alice's adventures are as fascinating now as they were when first published in 1865. The book's enormous success at the time gave other children's authors the confidence to stop concentrating solely on attempting to improve the young in their fiction. From now on, children's books could be entertaining and side more with the child. The image of

7 to 9

Alice answering back absurd adult characters with such robust good sense provided an extremely attractive figure for children, and became an example for other equally outspoken fictional child characters in years to come.

Hundreds of studies have been made of this story since it was published, each trying to work out exactly what it's really all about. Children themselves are rarely interested in such questions; instead, they want to know what happens next at particular moments, like the time when Alice grows much too tall and then later shrinks almost to invisibility. Some of the author's puns are not always easy to understand. But the comically ridiculous poems and the sense of being caught in a dream that occasionally turns into a nightmare is still attractive for many young readers. As is the array of bizarre but rounded characters – the White Rabbit, the Queen of Hearts or the Mad Hatter – who people its pages.

Films, pantomimes, plays and ballets have since been based on this extraordinary book, yet its true genius will always rest in the actual words Carroll used. The author knew how to communicate with children, in a period when many adults were distant and formal in their relationships with the young. Reading this book at any age is to surround oneself with images that may often only be half understood but still remain curiously fascinating. The sequel to this story, *Alice Through the Looking Glass*, also contains many marvellous moments

7 to 9

– although children usually seem to prefer the first volume.

Many different editions of this famous story now exist, but the original, which was illustrated by Sir John Tenniel under the critical eye of the author, still maintains its hold. For those children who find Tenniel a little forbidding, Helen Oxenbury's charming watercolours for Walker Books adopt a more modern approach with Alice very much a contemporary child.

## The Hobbit

**J.R.R. Tolkien** (author) **Alan Lee** (illustrator)
HarperCollins (hb & pb)

7 to 9

The author originally told a version of this story to his own children before eventually contacting a publisher who asked his son to read it. The verdict was favourable, and so one of the most celebrated of all children's stories was published in 1937. Never out of print since, it describes a timeless world of dwarves, elves, wizards, dragons and Tolkien's own invention, hobbits. These are people of about half-human height who wear bright clothes and live in comfortable burrows known as Hobbit-holes. Naturally good-humoured and pleasure loving, they are not really the stuff of warriors – least of all Bilbo Baggins, the fifty-year-old hero of this story. But when Gandalf the wizard tells Bilbo about his plan to raid the treasure hoard of Smaug – the fire-breathing dragon who lives in the middle of a mountain – the temptation is too much and Bilbo, along with a band of dwarves, starts out on what proves to be a highly eventful journey. On the way he and his friends have to deal with trolls, goblins and giant spiders, all potentially deadly enemies, while also coming across many other creatures who offer friendship.

The fascination of this story owes much to the author's total belief in what he was writing. His own maps and illustrations share space with poems and detailed descriptions of the dramatic scenery that the companions pass through on the way to confront the dragon. Some characters are both comic and menacing, such as old Gollum, a small, slimy creature "as dark as darkness, except for two big round pale eyes in his thin face". His mumblings and grumblings are much in evidence as the pace quickens in this extraordinary book.

The three-volume sequel, *The Lord of the Rings*, is recommended for older children in the next section, but *The Hobbit* is more clearly aimed at a younger audience, with the author often addressing them in a folksy and informal fashion. The heart of the story still remains the traditional tale of adventure (dating at least as far back as Beowulf) in which a group of friends brave hardships in order to hunt down and kill the monster that threatens the rest of their society. The author, a Professor of Anglo-Saxon, was an expert on such epics; it is the good fortune of children that he put so much of his knowledge into creating a story as exciting and compulsively readable as this one.

## Mary Poppins
**P.L. Travers** (author)
HarperCollins (pb)

A story about a children's nanny with a perpetual sniff could sound both old-fashioned and slightly off-putting. But this is to forget the enduring appeal of magic to children, a quality that Mary Poppins immediately reveals when she arrives at the home of the Banks family and slides up the banisters. To start with, only the children know about her extraordinary powers, giving them a secret that makes each day both unpredictable and exciting: they fly, talk to animals and eat the most amazing meals, all in the company of a nanny who may look disapproving but in reality allows them almost everything they want.

Although most child readers at this age will no longer believe in such magic themselves, they may still love imagining its possibilities. Because their imagination remains very powerful, they have fewer difficulties than adults when it comes to accepting stories, where the magic is set in an otherwise everyday world of streets and cars rather than in a remote fairyland. Indeed such is the attraction of this ordinary nanny with such extraordinary powers, that over the years many children have written to the author, begging her to arrange a meeting with Mary for themselves. She even once received a letter from a parent suggesting that because Mary "has really left the Banks family, couldn't she come to me?"

## More of Mary

Mary Poppins Comes Back

Mary Poppins Opens the Door

Mary Poppins in the Park

Mary Poppins and the House Next Door

Mary Poppins in Cherry Tree Lane

7 to 9

# Peter Pan and Wendy

**J.M. Barrie** (author) **Michael Foreman** (illustrator)
Pavilion (hb & pb)

The story of Peter Pan was originally written for the stage, where for years it played at theatres all over Britain during the Christmas holidays. Later on the author turned the play into a book which, though it may lack some of the excitement of a visit to the theatre, still has all the ingredients that made the play so successful. Peter, a boy who never grows up, visits the children of Mr and Mrs Darling – Wendy, John and Michael – in their bedroom at night where he teaches them to fly. Once the children have mastered the art, everyone rushes off to Neverland where, led by Peter and his fairy companion Tinkerbell, they rescue the Lost Boys, play games with mermaids and – best of all – fight with a gang of pirates led by the totally villainous Captain Hook.

All these adventures were based on games the author used to play with the five children from a family he first befriended and later looked after. So although the language used in the story often sounds quite violent, it is soon evident to a young audience that these are people who are only playing their parts. That is why the pirates themselves sometimes sound so childish, and why Captain Hook is always so gloriously over-the-top. Mr and Mrs Darling have little to do or say in the main

7 to 9

section of this story, just as parents are often absent from children's best imaginative games. But when the children do return home their loving parents are overjoyed to see them again. Only Peter maintains his independence to the last, making him that bit more memorable a hero.

## The Wind in the Willows

**Kenneth Grahame** (author) **E.H. Shepard** (illustrator)
Mammoth (hb & pb)

Like many of the best books for children, this one began as a story told by the author to one of his own children – in this case his small son – which later continued in letters when the boy went off on a holiday with his nurse. These letters, said to have been rescued from a wastepaper basket, went on to provide the core of this famous and much-loved story. Most of the

narrative originally focused on Toad, the most engaging rogue ever created in children's literature, whose faults include boastfulness, greed, dishonesty and a complete lack of self-discipline. But he is also good-hearted and (like Shakespeare's Falstaff) not only good-humoured in himself but also the cause of much good humour in others. Children might catch a glimpse of themselves in the way that he's regularly carried away by new enthusiasms, regardless of the circumstances. But they will also warm to the other characters in this book, such as the responsible Water-Rat, the shy but affectionate Mole and the stern but ever-reliable Badger.

The story begins on a lovely spring day, with Mole and Rat paying visits to each other and planning picnics together. Yet there is a constant threat in the air, summed up by the darkness of the Wild Wood, a lawless place where no responsible riverside animal would ever go alone – least of all at night. It is full of dangerous stoats and weasels who eventually seize Toad Hall after its owner is imprisoned for serious driving offences. Everything is settled by the end, but not before some genuinely exciting adventures. The book also contains sections where the author writes about his own devotion to nature, notably the chapter "The Piper at the Gates of Dawn", but these can easily be skipped by a young audience eager to get back to the fun and games surrounding Mr Toad. Various films have been

7 to 9

made of this story, and A.A. Milne also provided an effective stage version of it in his play *Toad of Toad Hall*, but the book itself is still supreme, with Toad himself one of the great figures of all literature.

## The Wind in the Willows Illustrated

**Ernest Shepard**'s drawings for *The Wind in the Willows*, which first appeared in 1930, seem so entirely appropriate for the book and its characters that it is surprising to learn that he was not the author's first choice. Kenneth Grahame actually wanted **Arthur Rackham**, who did eventually get round to illustrating an American edition in 1940. Both artists were concerned to capture the spirit of the book and visited Grahame's Thames-side home at Pangbourne. In Rackham's version, currently available as an Everyman hardback, the animals are less domestic and more wild than Shepard's, and overall there is a greater sense of danger. Since these two there have been many wonderful illustrated versions. Of those currently available, three stand out. **Michael Foreman**'s sumptuous watercolours can be found in a wide format edition for Pavilion; **Inga Moore**'s more detailed and intimate pictures illustrate an abridged version of the book for Walker; and **Patrick Benson**'s relatively cosy but extremely charming interpretation is published by HarperCollins.

7 to 9

# Animal Stories

These stories range from accounts of real animals to tales that describe animal characters who also possess human speech and understanding. Both types of story have always been popular, since children of this age group still possess a special feeling for animals, and often particularly enjoy stories that picture their own world from the point of view of a pet. Seeing oneself as others see us is a skill that may be slow to develop, yet children often take quickly to the idea that animals are watching and judging us. Criticism of human characters from an animal viewpoint can also be easier to accept than judgements made by grown-ups or by peers. But plenty of animal stories are mainly interested in telling a good tale, although even here there are frequent moments when animal characters desperately need to be listened to and understood by surrounding humans.

7 to 9

Such kindness and consideration for animals has not always been evident in the past, and there is no doubt that animal stories over the years have played an important part in changing children's own views and behaviour in this matter.

## Charlotte's Web
**E.B. White** (author) **Garth Williams** (illustrator)
Puffin (pb)

"'Where's Papa going with that axe?' said Fern to her mother as they were setting the table for breakfast." The answer she gets is anything but reassuring, and running into the pigpen Fern only just stops her farmer-father from slaughtering the smallest pig in the new litter. The tiny piglet, already pushed out by his bigger brothers and sisters, had not been expected to live for much longer anyway. But Fern is allowed to take him over, and with regular feeding he survives to become

Wilbur, a much loved pet. As he grows bigger and fatter he comes to realize that his own sudden death cannot much longer be avoided. But he reckons without Charlotte, a talking grey spider who lives in the corner of the same barn.

Wilbur is duly saved by a series of ingenious tricks and ruses, all thought up by Charlotte herself. At the same time this strange pair also have various conversations about numbers of important subjects, including death itself. Many children are often fascinated by this topic, and are sometimes more ready to talk openly about it than the adults in their company. But other children can occasionally become frightened by the whole idea of dying, and find it hard to discuss their private worries. This story brings into focus some of the fundamental issues of mortality in a gentle, good-humoured – and thoroughly unalarming – way. The author achieves this fine balance with wit and style; he also provides plenty of food for thought for young minds beginning to grapple with some of the complexities of existence, whether human or otherwise.

## The Hundred and One Dalmatians

**Dodie Smith** (author) **Janet & Anne Grahame** (illustrators)

Mammoth (pb)

Pongo and Missis are two Dalmatian dogs living

happily with their owners Mr and Mrs Dearly. But then enters Cruella de Vil – a lady quite as evil as any fairy-tale witch. Expelled from school for drinking ink, she now shows a most unhealthy interest in the Dalmatians' new litter of fifteen puppies. "Wouldn't they make enchanting fur coats?" she remarks to her husband, and before long all the puppies have been kidnapped by the equally sinister Baddun brothers, who run a Dalmatian fur farm. It is now up to Pongo and

Missis to win back their family before it is too late. Climbing to the top of London's Primrose Hill, they bark the canine equivalent of "Help!" to all other dogs within earshot. Within minutes the message about stolen puppies has been relayed across Britain, and at last the call comes back that they have been found.

What happens next is equally exciting and satisfying.

Dodie Smith was a successful novelist for older readers, and in this novel she demonstrates how well she could write for a younger audience too. She knew that children love a really evil villain, and although Cruella's menacing appearance occasionally proves too scary for some children when watching the Disney film version of the story, she is less monstrous here – though still just as nasty. Children particularly like the idea of animals clubbing together for a common cause as they do in this marvellous story. The author also raises issues about the way society treats animals, which some children may want to talk about this afterwards. Others will be content to bask in the pleasure of a good story expertly told.

## The Owl Tree

**Jenny Nimmo** (author) **Anthony Lewis** (illustrator)
Walker (pb)

Visiting his great-grandmother while his mother is expecting a baby, Joe becomes entranced by the huge tree growing in a neighbour's garden. A rare barn owl is nesting at the top, but the neighbour – nicknamed "monster" because of his strange discoloured face – denies there's an owl up there and resolves to chop the tree down. Joe knows he has to save the tree, since the prospect of it disappearing is badly affecting his

great-grandmother, who has got used to the view over the years and cannot bear to lose it. One way would be to climb the tree and discover the owl for himself, but how can he do this when he's terrified of heights?

This short book is reminiscent of a late nineteenth-century classic *The Gentle Heritage* by Frances E. Crompton. In both novels a lonely, disfigured neighbour is brought back into the community by the actions of small children who are able to see the essential humanity that exists beneath their off-putting appearance. Jenny Nimmo also adds an ecological dimension, with the Owl Tree becoming a character in its own right when it seems to share some of the human feelings going on around it. Line drawings by Anthony Lewis add a compelling atmosphere to a story, which moves from quite ordinary experiences to a more mystical feeling for nature itself. Although the owl in question plays a comparatively minor role, the strong emotions it rouses cover a range of symbolic meanings, from nostalgia for the past to that sense of freedom often associated with wild animals.

7 to 9

## The Sheep-Pig
**Dick King-Smith** (author) **Mike Terry** (illustrator)
Puffin (pb)

Pig characters in animal stories have often posed

children's writers with something of a problem. While other farmyard animals exist for reasons other than their meat alone, pigs are there simply to be eaten, and however lovable they may seem (especially

when young), in real life they have no way of avoiding this fate as they grow older. Many children's books get round this by depicting pigs living an amiable, trouble-free existence, but these tend to be written for younger children. Older readers, by contrast, will often be more cynical about soft answers in their stories – whether featuring pigs or anything else.

But Dick King-Smith, like E.B. White in *Charlotte's Web*, meets this problem without flinching in a charming story, later made into the hugely popular film *Babe*. Farmer Hogget and his wife have every intention of slaughtering their little pig Babe when the time comes, and all the other farmyard animals know this too except for Babe himself. The way in which he avoids this fate forms the main plot of the rest of the story, but with plenty more thrown in besides. By

7 to 9

treating the sheep with greater respect, in his career as an alternative sheepdog, Babe is rewarded with greater co-operation. And by refusing to accept that only dogs can work sheep, Farmer Hogget also stands up for individual freedom, choice and respect. Add an exciting adventure with rustlers, a near-fatal misunderstanding and a final triumph against all the odds and this is a book likely to remain a firm favourite with children for a long time.

## Woof!

**Allan Ahlberg** (author) **Fritz Wegner** (illustrator)
Puffin (pb)

7 to 9

Eric Banks seems a perfectly ordinary boy. But one evening just after he has gone to bed he changes into a Norfolk terrier. When his parents discover him next morning they think he's some strange dog who has got in the house and shoo him out. His only hope after that is his best friend Roy Ackerman, but how can Eric communicate properly when all he can do is bark?

This is the fascinating proposition suggested in this story by Allan Ahlberg, one of the best and most innovative modern writers for the young. Children have always been fascinated by the idea of changing into animals, as in the many fairy tales where this happens. But the author reminds readers of some of the disadvantages: Eric, for instance, soon has to learn to walk behind his friend Roy because of the risk of being hit by a pram, "which was a hazard like a tank for a dog his size". He is also always afraid of being trodden on, and the dust on the pavement gives him a perpetual thirst. But there are gains as well: when his baby sister is lost he can easily trace her by following her scent. Eric finally goes back to being a boy for good, except by this time he is ready for the next bewildering

change in his life – from childhood to adolescence. This is a thoughtful as well as a very funny story which all children should enjoy, whether they have a pet dog or not.

# Fantasy Stories

7 to 9

Fantasy stories are particularly appropriate for an age group where the imagination is still so strong that suspending disbelief is rarely a problem. Most of these stories take place in a recognisable human world made much more interesting by regular injections of applied magic. Other tales present purely imaginary worlds peopled by equally fantastic characters. Children themselves are often adept at inventing their own pretend worlds, sometimes of quite extraordinary complexity. So it is no particular problem for them to accept someone else's imaginary landscape in the course of a story, so long as it is described well enough and the adventures that happen there are memorable. All the stories included here pass this test, and very soon young readers will find themselves accepting the bizarre occurrences that happen within them as if these are everyday events. Many of the best fantasy writers are also describing the real state of the world as they see it but employing symbolism and magic instead of realism in order to make their points.

## The Borrowers Aloft
**Mary Norton** (author) **Diana Stanley** (illustrator)
Puffin (pb)

All those little things so easily lost in any household are in fact taken by the Borrowers, tiny people who live under the floorboards and only come out at night. They have to live too, and humans are usually able to spare the odd crumb of food, button, coin or anything else Pod, Homily and their daughter Arrietty can put to such good use. When in *The Borrowers Aloft* – the best of the series – the family come across a tiny model village built by an old man as a hobby, the unfamiliar

comfort it offers is just too tempting. They move in, but despite being extremely careful they are eventually spotted by two humans, who promptly decide to kidnap them in order to turn them into the world's most exciting exhibition. While their new quarters are being built, the family makes plans for escape involving a homemade balloon. But time is desperately short, and their human enemies are cunning as well as greedy.

The author wrote five books about these tiny people who look and behave exactly like ordinary humans except for having to survive in an oversized world where even spiders seem like formidable opponents. Such characters can have a special meaning for children, themselves familiar with the problems of living in an environment where everything seems too big. But Mary Norton also introduces some of the normal familial tensions that arise when a spirited only child lives with parents who are beginning to become a little elderly and over-cautious. There is also some love interest for Arrietty, plus the endless fascination of seeing how the small can and do eventually outwit the large.

## All the Borrowers

The Borrowers
The Borrowers Afield
The Borrowers Afloat

The Borrowers Aloft
The Borrowers Avenged

## The Earth Giant
**Melvin Burgess** (author)
Andersen Press (hb) Puffin (pb)

One night a fierce storm topples a mighty oak tree.
Under its roots, seven-year-old Amy discovers a slowly
awakening female giant, about four metres tall and a
mixture of human and
animal. Although the
giant has no speech,
Amy always knows
what she is thinking,
and regularly brings
her food in her new
hiding place at a
disused cinema. But
older brother Peter
follows his sister on her
journey there one
night, after which
everything falls apart.
The giant runs away
with Amy, and Peter
gets the blame for not
telling his parents all he
knew. In a desperate, last twist of the plot, both
children defy their parents once again to help the giant,
who turns out to be no more than a child herself. She

7 to 9

finally escapes to another planet on a spacecraft manned by her even taller parents.

Melvin Burgess is a writer never afraid to tackle important themes, and this often rather sombre story concentrates on the problems of alienation felt first by the giant and then by the children who try to help her. Every character has moments of suffering, from the giant herself to her anxious young helpers and their own parents, sick with worry when they discover their daughter is missing. But there are lighter moments as well, when the giant takes the children out for moonlit runs at enormous speed. Burgess is always a stimulating writer, easy to read while leaving plenty to think about afterwards. *The Earth Giant* is a good case in point. Genuinely thought-provoking as well as continually gripping, it is also aimed at children ready to take on some more serious themes in fiction.

**7 to 9**

## Finn Family Moomintroll
**Tove Jansson** (author/illustrator)
Puffin (pb)

Moomins are small, fat and shy creatures who hibernate for a hundred days when the snows come. They live in Moomin Valley, Moominland – defined by the author as a place where "everyone did what they liked and seldom worried about tomorrow". A mixture

of human and animal, the chief character is
Moomintroll, son of Moominpapa – always depicted
wearing a top hat – and Moominmamma, a character
inseparable from her capacious handbag. Friends
include Sniff, who looks a bit like a kangaroo; Snufkin,
a goggle-eyed manikin who plays a mouth organ; and
the Hemulen, a male who regularly wears a dress. One
mild adventure follows another, with rides on passing

clouds followed by a
mini-disaster when the
hot-tempered Muskrat,
who is also a
philosopher, feels that
his precious dignity has
been irreparably
damaged when his
hammock collapses.

Reading this book is
rather like watching
one of those absorbing
games small children
play with stuffed toys,
where each character
has its own part in an imaginary setup known and
understood only by those playing at the time. Jansson's
gentle stories have a similarly hypnotic quality as one
strange incident follows another, to be commented on
by whichever weird creature happens to be on the page

at that moment. But the author (who, although Finnish, wrote in Swedish) never descends into mere whimsy. She also has a sly wit much in evidence in the frequent passages of dialogue, which at times reach the same inspired level of inconsequentiality found in A.A. Milne's stories about Christopher Robin and Pooh Bear. Her black-and-white illustrations extend the mood of dreamy, affectionate fantasy found throughout this book and its various sequels – all of which have been popular with young readers throughout Europe for the last fifty years.

## Haroun and the Sea of Stories

**Salman Rushdie** (author) **Paul Birkbeck** (illustrator)

Penguin (hb & pb)

7 to 9

This modern fairy story features Rashid the storyteller, the so-called Shah of Blah, and his son Haroun. They live in a small concrete house midway between the skyscrapers of the super-rich and the tumbledown shacks of the destitute in a country which is never identified but which has much in common with modern-day India. Both characters are named after the legendary Caliph of Baghdad, Haroun al-Rashid, who appears in many of the original *Tales of the Arabian Nights*. Their story starts one terrible day when Haroun's mother disappears with another man, leaving her husband too depressed to tell any more tales for his living. In desperation Haroun flies on the back of a Hoopoe bird to the fabulous Sea of Stories in search of the Story Waters that will enable his father to start recounting his tales again. There he meets many bizarre creatures living strange lives in fabulous surroundings. All ends happily, with Haroun's family finally restored to what it was and the sad city where they live at last returning to some sense of joy.

As a fantasy, this is very much one for our own times, describing dishonest politicians, polluting factories and many other of the less desirable features of modern life. As in the original *Tales of the Arabian Nights*, there is a cast of extraordinary characters involved in completely unpredictable adventures. The author's exuberant way with language gives the text some of the immediacy of a story told within a family by a parent who is never

too sure what exactly is going to happen next. Thrilling illustrations by Paul Birkbeck add to this imaginative feast, where danger and the suggestion of cruelty are never far away. There is also a constant promise of colour and excitement, accompanied by the type of broad humour young readers particularly like.

## Harry Potter and the Philosopher's Stone

**J.K. Rowling** (author)

Bloomsbury (hb & pb)

**7 to 9**

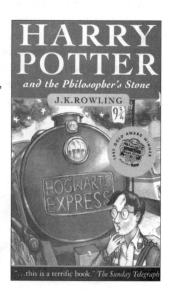

Harry Potter is an orphan who lives with a horrible uncle, aunt and cousin – all of whom make his life a misery. But everything changes when he is whisked away to Hogwarts School of Witchcraft and Wizardry, which both his parents had attended before him. Harry is immediately recognized as

"...this is a terrific book." *The Sunday Telegraph*

someone special by the scar on his forehead, the product of a terrible battle that took place where both his parents died saving his life when he was still a baby. Although soon he makes some good friends, there are also some powerful enemies who seem to know more about Harry and what he represents than he does himself. While life at Hogwarts remains continually interesting, with all types of magic taking place as everyday occurrences, there are also moments when Harry's very existence is in danger. In order to survive, he has to find great qualities of courage – with the effort involved sometimes stretching him almost to breaking point.

Such are the bare bones of this now famous story, with its successors falling into fairly similar patterns with Harry a year older in each sequel. Their huge success with readers young and old is well-deserved, given that there is always so much here to entertain as well as occasionally disturb. Harry himself has the appeal of a Cinderella character: everything is initially against him but he triumphs in the end. Popular with his friends and with most of his teachers, he is also extraordinarily talented at the game of quidditch, a type of aerial lacrosse played on flying broomsticks. Success or failure at this game is highly prized, and the way Harry regularly manages to win the cup for his comrades in Gryffindor House is reminiscent of similar triumphs found in traditional boarding school stories.

7 to 9

But in other ways these tales make a distinct break from previous models. Lessons are solely occupied with learning magical skills rather than with bothering about orthodox academic subjects, and magic has a way of breaking out in the most unexpected places so that even a door or a staircase is capable of springing the odd surprise. Ghosts are a part of everyday life, some more malignant than others, and selected animals have special skills undreamt of in the natural world.

All these ingredients are held together by a writer who knows how to tell a good story. Suspense is kept up until the last page, and in between there are sometimes as many good jokes on one page as there are in whole books by less talented authors. Villains remain suitably villainous, but even here things may not always be what they seem, with Harry occasionally discovering that he has been quite mistaken about certain characters. Although he is a remarkably resourceful child there are moments when he nearly despairs, reminding readers that he is also a very human hero rather than a junior superman. And at the end of one adventure there is always another one to turn to or reread, with the whole saga planned to end with volume seven (four have appeared so far). Rowling is not an innovative writer, and children should always be encouraged to try out other books that might sometimes seem more challenging, but for sheer entertainment value she is hard to beat.

## The Indian in the Cupboard
**Lynne Reid Banks** (author) **Piers Sanford** (illustrator)
HarperCollins (pb)

Omri is not that delighted when his older brother
presents him with a small secondhand plastic model of
a Red Indian as a birthday present. But putting this
figure into a bathroom cupboard has the unexpected
effect of bringing him to life as Little Bull, the son of an
Iroquois chief. This character, barely two inches high,
starts by ordering Omri around like a servant, but
when Omri supplies him with a horse which has also
come to life in the cupboard, relations improve. Omri
starts to find out more about the Iroquois while at
school, but things get even more complicated when his
younger brother gets in on the act and brings a toy
cowboy called Boone to life as well. A genuine cowboy
and Indian fight is followed by a reconciliation after
which Omri finally returns them both to the bathroom

cupboard where they turn into plastic figures once again.

This ingenious story has intrigued many children since it was first published in 1981. Little Bull is not simply a child's fantasy of a perfect secret friend, since he is also imperious, aggressive and quite difficult to live with. But these very faults are made to seem quite understandable as he develops into one of those characters continually obsessed with trying to maintain a fierce but sometimes fragile pride. This is not easy when he is also under the control of a giant schoolboy. Rather like a wild animal that gradually accepts some human rules, Little Bull's final admission of friendship with Omri is all the more moving because it has been so hard-won. His quarrels with the cowboy Boone meanwhile symbolize some of the realities of American nineteenth-century history, and touch on the experience of its indigenous people. Children who know about these events from the cowboy's point of view will come across a rather different version here. They will also learn

7 to 9

158

something about the mystery of human relations as the two warring figures finally resolve their difficulties. Best of all, young readers will experience the full power of an excellent story and the way that a skilled author can make even the most unlikely of scenarios come alive.

### More Tales of the Indian

## The Last Giants
**François Place** (author/illustrator)
Pavilion (pb)

7 of 9

This haunting fantasy, written by a Belgian author who provides his own inspired watercolour illustrations, describes the imaginary journey of a nineteenth-century British explorer to the Land of the Giants. He finds out about this lost region after acquiring from an old sailor an outsize tooth on which a tiny map is inscribed. Setting sail with all his provisions on board, the explorer travels as far as Burma and then sails down the Black River. After losing his companions to the bloodthirsty Wa tribe, the explorer finally makes it alone to giant territory. There he meets and finally

**7 to 9**

becomes friends with its small community of peaceful, vast and century-old inhabitants for a year before returning home. But telling others about his exploits once he is back has tragic results, with the gentle giants eventually killed off by unscrupulous treasure-hunters looking for immediate profit.

All these events are recounted so soberly that readers could almost believe that this is a true story. The accompanying illustrations also contain enough period detail to keep young eyes happily employed every time the book is picked up. But this story is far more than a skilled pastiche of an old travel journal. It is also a parable about exploitation – whether of humans, animals or of the earth itself. Although they are so huge, the giants are no match for their much smaller human predators. Living harmoniously with each other, they never develop the aggressive cunning necessary to survive in more hostile surroundings. As such, they are in complete contrast to the murderous, thieving type of giant familiar from fairy tales. But these figures are big in spirit as well as in size, and although the end of their story is sad many children will still be fascinated by the very idea of such creatures. They may also respond to the story's eloquent message about the importance of tolerance and understanding.

## The Lion, the Witch and the Wardrobe

**C.S. Lewis** (author) **Pauline Baynes** (illustrator)

HarperCollins (hb & pb)

Four children have been evacuated during World War II to a strange house in the countryside. One of them, Lucy, discovers that she can travel through the back of a wardrobe into a country of snow and pine forests known as Narnia. But when her brother Edmund tries to join her, he runs straight into the White Witch, a tyrant feared throughout the whole of the land. Tempted by her promise of unending Turkish Delight – his favourite sweet – Edmund becomes her servant. It is now up to the others to release him from this enchantment, and to rid Narnia of the witch and the rest of her evil empire for ever. This they eventually achieve with the help of Aslan, a gentle but in every other way masterful lion who, like some other animals in Narnia, also possesses powers of human speech and understanding.

The author created this story because, in his own words, "People won't write the books I want, so I have to do it for myself." And as this classic work of fiction makes clear, the type of book he wanted was one that used fairy-tale imagery to introduce children to a Christian message. He does this so subtly that many readers, child and adult, enjoy this story without ever realizing that Aslan in fact stands for Christ while the White Witch – so expert in seeking out human weaknesses – is also the Devil. When Aslan gives himself up to the White Witch as part of a bargain to save Edmund, he is killed on a stone table after being bound and having his mane shorn off. This humiliating and cruel punishment is a symbol of the Crucifixion; but it is followed soon after by the Resurrection, when

Aslan returns to life and the White Witch is finally vanquished.

Had this book been written for children in the nineteenth century, the biblical imagery would no doubt have been made much clearer throughout. But by 1950 when it first appeared the author knew that any overt preaching could well lose him most of his audience. He settled instead for a tale that draws on a Christian story for its foundation but which functions in its own right as an epic adventure. He also borrows from many of the great myths familiar to him through his work as a university teacher of Medieval English. Finally, there is some dipping into the more recent past as well: the occupants of Narnia, for example, are shown going through the same terrors experienced in Europe during World War II – still a recent memory for older child readers at the time.

Critics have been divided in their response to this book and its six sequels. Some dislike the continued emphasis upon violence as a way of settling quarrels, with Father Christmas – enlisted here on the side of the good – at one point depicted handing out weapons before one of the many battles. Others insist that this story is in the great tradition of epic writing, providing young readers with an unforgettable and inspiring glimpse of a world where personal courage and the ability to make the right moral choices can still ensure that final victory is always possible. Children themselves usually enjoy this book, relishing its sense of high drama as they are whirled along by an author who is an expert storyteller. The same is generally true of their response to the other books in the Narnia sequence – except perhaps for *The Last Battle*, the final link in the chain. This takes place in an afterlife to which all the child characters have been transported after having unknowingly died in a rail crash, but many feel that the author's attempts to reassure young readers that this is still all for the best never really worked. But *The Lion, the Witch and the Wardrobe*, the first to be written and still the most successful story of the sequence, remains equal to Hans Andersen's tales in its power to evoke a mysterious other world. It also has a vivid sense of a continuing adventure where the stakes are high and there is no place for the timid, as the final confrontation between the powers of good and evil slowly but inexorably draws near.

## The Chronicles of Narnia

The Magician's Nephew

The Lion, the Witch and the Wardrobe

The Horse and His Boy

Prince Caspian

The Voyage of the Dawn Treader

The Silver Chair

The Last Battle

**7 to 9**

## Only You Can Save Mankind

**Terry Pratchett** (author)

Corgi (pb)

As the mighty alien fleet from the latest computer game thunders across the screen, Johnny prepares to blow up as many space vehicles as possible – until suddenly a surprising message appears in front of his eyes: "We Surrender". Just in time, Johnny realizes that there are real people out there who do not want to die. To save them he has to get inside the screen himself, but this also makes him a target for other trigger-happy players.

Terry Pratchett is well known to readers of all ages for his very successful Discworld stories. More than any other writer, he bridges the gap between books and the video screen, equally at home with either and brilliant at linking them. *Only You Can Save Mankind* is thoughtful as well as exciting, for once allowing the aliens some of the best lines while making the human world seem the one that is violent and unreasoning. The whole concept of a "reversed viewpoint" has a long history in children's literature, and provides children with an unfamiliar and interesting way of looking at themselves – and others – from an entirely different point of view. Here it's the figures in the video screen who come alive with thoughts and feelings of their own. It's a brilliant device, and the final humanitarian message is all the more powerful for having been

7 to 9

delivered by an author of such great popularity with the young. It should also be pointed out that this novel is extremely funny and does an excellent job of reproducing the kind of backchat that children share among themselves.

## Pippi Longstocking

**Astrid Lindgren** (author) **Chris Riddell** (illustrator)
Puffin (pb)

The heroine of these stories is only nine years old but already has sufficient strength to lift and carry her own horse unaided. She lives by herself in a little cottage, where Tommy and Annika first meet her. These two children from ordinary homes are soon bowled over by her unconventional lifestyle, which is spent overcoming the local bullies, evading the police (who want to put her in an orphanage) and behaving way beyond the rules of the local school she only visits for a day. Pippi represents every child's dream of independence, shamelessness and superhuman strength. But although she is often abrupt she has a warm heart, making it impossible for anyone to be angry with her for too long – except perhaps for the various baddies she always manages to outwit.

Originally published in 1945 and followed by many sequels, these stories featured the first heroine of children's literature to step outside a stereotyped view of girls, whether in real life or fiction. Claiming a mother who is an angel and a father who is a Cannibal King, Pippi herself is in some ways similar to Peter Pan, belonging both to this world and to somewhere else at the same time. Her occasional coarseness and bad manners constituted another breakthrough at a time when most child characters in fiction were still expected to set a good example to their young readers. The particular way she mangles words and phrases, one of her most popular characteristics in her native Sweden, presents translators with a difficult task – but not an impossible one, as this translation by Edna Hurup testifies. Lively new drawings by Chris Riddell, reinforce the image of Pippi as

a consistently happy and friendly child, content to be seen wearing her usual outfit of a patched home-made dress, odd stockings and men's shoes that are twice her size. For children, she is the ideal imaginary friend – resourceful, always up to something and completely uncowed by every aspect of the adult world. Famous all over Europe and the star of a number of films, she is

one of the most original and enjoyable characters found in all twentieth-century children's fiction. The many other Pippi books include *Pippi Goes Abroad* and *Pippi in the South Seas*.

## Stig of the Dump

**Clive King** (author) **Edward Ardizzone** (illustrator)
Puffin (pb)

Barney is a solitary child, who likes wandering off in the surrounding countryside by himself while on holiday with his grandparents. One day at the bottom of an old chalk pit he discovers not just a hidden cave but someone living in it "with a lot of shaggy hair and two bright black eyes". This turns out to be Stig, a stone-age boy dressed in rabbit-skins and speaking only in grunts. But the two boys soon learn to understand each other, and set about

improving Stig's cave by adding a chimney made of tin cans. Other adventures follow, including an occasion where they outwit some burglars who have raided Barney's house and another time where they rescue an escaped leopard. Barney tries to tell his grandparents about Stig, but they think he is simply describing an imaginary friend and do not take him seriously.

Stig is in fact very much the sort of companion children might make up for themselves, and so too are the various adventures the two have together. The fact that Stig comes from prehistoric times means he is completely out of the normal childhood experience of school, clean clothes, regular meals and life in a house under close parental supervision. Instead, he and Barney can play to their heart's content, since Stig lives by his own rules and answers to no one but himself. This image of freedom, within which two boys are seen to be able to do almost whatever they like, makes this one of the best stories about friendship there has ever been. Written with a light touch and accompanied by delightful illustrations by Edward Ardizzone, these happy adventures make excellent reading for children, particularly at times when they might otherwise feel bored by the events in their real lives. The author has written many other books for children, including his delightful *Me and My Million*, which describes a boy who unexpectedly comes across a picture worth a huge amount of money and does not know what to do next.

7 to 9

## Unbelievable!

**Paul Jennings** (author)

Puffin (pb)

Anything can happen in the weird and wacky world of Paul Jennings. In this collection of short stories, a small transistor makes people grow younger or older in just a few moments, sometimes ending up as babies or skeletons if they don't take their finger off the controls in time. There is also some revolting new toothpaste that causes teeth to grow to giant-size, while in other

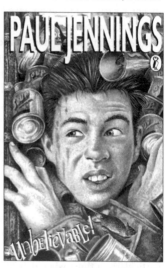

stories an exploration of the drains involves finding the body of a dead dragon, birds who manage to bury a house overnight with their droppings and a pair of eyes which look out from inside a milk bottle. And so it goes on; this particular title is just one of many collections

7 to 9

of tales written by Paul Jennings, all very funny and with a large chunk of yucky detail thrown in.

Children have always enjoyed tall stories as well as a fair share of the gruesome; Paul Jennings likes to combine both ingredients in his fiction and has been doing this so successfully since 1985 that over two million copies of his books have been sold. Adults may not always be so keen, but children should always be allowed their own reasons for having favourite books, even if they are unclear themselves as to what these reasons are.

7 to 9

# Adventure Stories

Adventure stories are always very popular with this age group. Tales where heroic individuals usually win through at the last moment, often against difficult odds, have an obvious meaning for children, given that reading about others performing brave or wonderful deeds is always a good deal easier than trying to perform such deeds in real life. But there is still a need to test oneself out at this age, if only in the imagination, and the adventure stories recommended here often test the characters involved to the limit. Some of the stories are also very funny, but behind the laughs there is still usually a strong, satisfying story involving courage, resourcefulness and the final defeat of whatever villains are involved. Other stories take themselves more seriously, for those moods when young readers want to submerge themselves utterly in what is going on, keeping up a mood of total belief from start to finish. Most of the books recommended here also have many sequels, promising more hours of delight for those who already find the originals so deeply satisfying.

## Asterix
**René Goscinny** (author) **Albert Uderzo** (illustrator)
Orion (hb)

The cartoon character Asterix has for years proved particularly popular with male readers of all ages. The society in which he lives is itself almost wholly male, with a pronounced emphasis upon fighting, eating and general carousing. Women characters, when they exist, generally get on with the household chores and little else – unless they are young and beautiful, in which case they are allowed to walk around the village looking decorative and perhaps carrying a few flowers. The central theme of the series is a celebration of one tiny corner of Brittany which supposedly never surrendered to the otherwise all-conquering Romans. The reason given for this continued defiance is that the Gauls who lived there were truly mighty fighters, with none mightier than Asterix, a shrewd warrior of no great

7 to 9

physique but who gets his huge strength from drinking a magic potion supplied to him by the local Druid Getafix. His constant companion Obelix is also massively strong and a famous consumer of wild boar. Together the two men have many adventures, always returning in the end to their peaceful village ruled over by Vitalstatistix, chief of the tribe.

As the names involved suggest, these stories are comical – packed with puns, anachronisms and a series of running gags. Illustrated in comic-book style, the characters concerned are essentially caricatures who talk in the manner of whatever set of contemporaries are being satirized at the time. *Asterix in Britain*, for example, takes on the British, who though depicted as primitives are shown as having already developed some curious habits like tea-drinking and a love of neat little lawns. While younger readers will also get some of these surface jokes, there is plenty to satisfy them at a deeper level. Asterix himself is one more example of the little man who commands universal respect. The strong bond between him and Obelix reminds young readers of the close friendships some of them will be having at this age. The constant preoccupation with food and fighting in these pages (allied to a lack of interest in sex or romance), also tends to reflect the priorities of children – particularly male ones – at this age.

Pictures running across every page offer a commentary on what is going on in the text, with particularly important words often picked out in bold with lots of exclamation marks. For many British children, these stories may be the only translated French literature they ever come across. Their wit, energy and sheer inventiveness make them excellent advertisments for their country; they also show young readers that the British do not hold a monopoly on the type of fierce nationalism both mocked and celebrated within these pages.

## Another Six Asterix

Asterix and the Black Gold

Asterix and the Great Divide

Asterix and Son

Asterix and the Secret Weapon

Asterix and the Actress

Asterix and Obelix All At Sea

# Emil and the Detectives
**Erich Kästner** (author) **Walter Trier** (illustrator)
Red Fox (pb)

Emil sets out on a train journey by himself to stay with his aunt and grandmother in Berlin. Although his precious holiday money is pinned to his pocket through the lining of his jacket, it somehow disappears when he nods off for a few moments, the obvious thief

being a man in a bowler hat who was sitting opposite him on the train and who seemed rather suspicious.

Emil and his mother have little enough cash anyway, so he is determined to get the money back. This he does with the help of a group of Berlin boys and a girl, all of whom are around the same age. With every member of this newly-formed gang playing their part in some adept detective work, the thief is finally run to ground and Emil picks up a large reward. All that remains now is a large tea party given by his proud grandmother and attended by all his new friends.

This story, first published in 1931, has always proved a winner with children, even during World War II when many things German were under suspicion (the author himself was a prominent anti-Nazi). It owes its success to its brilliant realization of the childhood dream of a perfect gang, where everyone is seen working together in harmony without any need of adult help or intervention. The gang in this story is made up of a hundred working-class children whose street knowledge and independence makes them more than a match for any adult thief. But this is no anonymous, undifferentiated grouping, since selected children within it are also described as individuals each with his or her own particular characteristics. The way they are all so ready to help the stoical Emil is part of the optimistic image of childhood running through this book. Children know that in real life nothing would ever be quite as easy or positive as this, but it is always nice to dream. This story, with its quirky black-and-white illustrations by the famous German artist Walter Trier, was the forerunner to many other tales where children are shown solving mysteries and defeating criminals without adult help. But none of those published since has ever been quite as good as this little classic, which rates as one of the best adventure stories for children ever written.

## Five on a Treasure Island
**Enid Blyton** (author) **Eileen Soper** (illustrator)
Hodder (hb & pb)

An island, a ruined castle, a submerged wreck and a desperate hunt for buried gold ingots form the background to this first and best of Enid Blyton's adventure stories. The so-called Famous Five – two

boys, two girls and a dog – are allowed almost total freedom from adult control as they rush to seek out some buried treasure ahead of a gang of crooks. Briefly imprisoned in the castle's dungeons, the child adventurers are always going to be too clever and resourceful for any grown-ups foolish enough to stand in their way. The book ends as always with a chorus of praise for every one of the gallant band, plus the promise of more adventures to come. In fact Blyton went on to write twenty more Famous Five adventures in addition to the large quantity of other stories she produced in her lifetime.

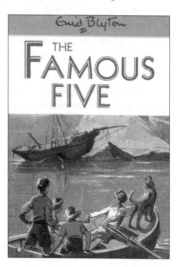

There was a time when Blyton was widely condemned for her repetitive use of language, unlikely plots and shallow characterization. Some parents who saw their children devouring this author at the expense of other,

7 to 9

more interesting, writers sometimes despaired of her influence. Although she is less popular now than she was, her stories are still widely read in editions that have often been brought up-to-date since they were first published. Although never a great writer, she possessed a marked ability to forge ahead with a story and was never afraid to tell readers just what a good time they must all be having.

Her plots are always totally unlikely, but they are very close to how children of this age group often wish that things might be in their daydreams. No other author has ever got as close to the make-believe world of a child in those moods when they like imagining that everything they do – either by themselves or else as part of a gang – proves ultimately successful whatever the odds. For this gift alone, Blyton deserves recognition for writing stories so child-oriented that the adults in them, apart from a few necessary villains, have almost nothing to do.

Millions of contented readers have enjoyed these stories, until they finally get too old for them, at which point they start noticing some of the faults that have always bothered Blyton's critics. While children today may be faster at getting to this point than were previous generations from a less sophisticated period, they should not be denied the chance of discovering something of the heady excitement that comes from reading a Blyton adventure story as hectic and action-packed as this one.

## Another Five Famous Five

| | |
|---|---|
| Five Go Adventuring Again | Smuggler's Top |
| Five on Finniston Farm | Five Get Into a Fix |
| Five Go Off to | Five On Kirrin Island Again |

## Tintin

**Hergé** (author/illustrator)

Mammoth (hb & pb)

**7 to 9**

There are twenty-one Tintin books in all, each illustrated to the same high standard of comic-strip art by one of the twentieth century's masters of the genre. The stories themselves are always fast-moving and exciting, driven by characters who – however comic at times – are also serious players in the melodramas going on around them. Chief among them is that amazingly resourceful junior reporter, Tintin himself with his characteristic blond quiff and old-fashioned plus-four trousers. Of indeterminate age – sometimes a child, at other times clearly adolescent – Tintin is regularly accompanied by Snowy, his faithful white terrier. As in all the best daydreams, Snowy is more than just a dog; he is a companion with a deep understanding of his master, whom he frequently has to rescue. Other regular characters are Captain Haddock,

Tintin's irascible but well-meaning friend; the Thomson twins, Europe's most inefficient detectives; and the unworldly Professor Calculus who is always working on some new invention or other. Readers meeting them in one story will encounter them in others too, always behaving according to type.

As with the Asterix stories, comic-strip art is always likely to be popular with younger readers since the pictures themselves tell a great deal of the story, leaving the ground clear for a fairly simple text. The  early stories make a point of visiting faraway locations, depicted in all their exotic splendour. This geographical interest is always there in Hergé's meticulously drawn and carefully-researched pictures, though in later volumes he focuses more on plot.

However dangerous the situations Tintin finds himself in, good humour is never far away – especially when the Thomson twins make one of their typically blundering appearances. These two characters, together

7 to 9

with the impulsive and easily-duped Captain Haddock, are always far less competent than Tintin himself and young readers are able to enjoy identifying with a hero so much more mature than his elders. Opportunities for feeling patronizing about selected adult characters provide children with the chance of getting their own back – at least in the imagination – on all those adults who in real life can seem like formidable authority figures. But there is more to Tintin than mere wish-fulfilment; the excitement of science and new technology also play a large role in these stories. Books that are so alive with energy have an important role for children, suggesting to them the fascination of the world they live in and how one day they too might be able to explore some of the faraway places that Tintin gets to visit.

## Ten of the Best Tintin Books

| | |
|---|---|
| Tintin in Tibet | The Castafiore Emerald |
| The Black Island | Prisoners of the Sun |
| Destination Moon | Tintin in America |
| King Ottakar's Sceptre | The Seven Crystal Balls |
| Red Rackham's Treasure | Land of Black Gold |

# Historical
# Stories

Younger children tend to live very much in the present, but at this age there can be a genuine curiosity about what life may have been like in past times and different circumstances. For most children, history starts and finishes only as far back as their parents or grandparents remember from their own lives. It can therefore be extremely stimulating for them to encounter other worlds far more distant and remote than those afforded by ageing family photographs and oft-repeated stories. Writers of historical fiction have the difficult task of trying to get some idea of the past over to readers while using mostly contemporary language at the same time. The best achieve this by devising a form of dialogue that is

both different from what might be heard today yet clear in its meaning at the same time. Illustrations can help here, with visual impressions sometimes more powerful than words in getting across a genuine atmosphere of the unfamiliar.

## The Cuckoo Tree

**Joan Aiken** (author) **Pat Marriott** (illustrator)

Red Fox (pb)

**7 to 9**

This is a history story with a difference, since here is an author who mixes historical truth with wild invention of her own. She describes a Britain in which the supporters of the Hanoverian monarchs are secretly plotting to kill the new King Richard the Fourth at his coronation. To do this they intend to plunge St Paul's Cathedral into the Thames after sliding it down Ludgate Hill on hidden giant rollers. All this is discovered by Dido Twite, a cockney girl of around twelve, who is so resourceful and streetwise that no adult villains – and there are plenty in these pages –

have any real hope of outwitting her. Throw in a couple of witches, a kidnapping and a vital dispatch that has to get to London in time, and you have a story brimming with excitement.

By playing with history in this way, Joan Aiken hopes to make it seem rather more fun than the official version taught in school. That is why she goes in for crazy ideas such as an early channel tunnel through which wolves come over to Britain from Europe, not to mention an eighteenth-century train complete with a billiard room carriage. Choosing a historical time when children did not have to go to school and where communications were still difficult has many other advantages for a children's writer: her young characters, for example, must make long and dangerous journeys in order to deliver vital messages. High adventure ensues, with various wicked characters doing their worst before finally getting their comeuppance. The dialogue in this story uses a number of imaginary words and phrases, but these are always easy to understand – while often very funny in their own right.

The author has written several other stories involving Dido Twite, starting with the popular *The Wolves of Willoughby Chase*, but they are not planned as a sequence and all stand on their own. Joan Aiken is always firmly on the side of her young characters, and is expert at creating the sort of melodrama which is always gripping but that never takes itself too seriously.

## I Am David

**Anne Holm** (author)

Mammoth (pb)

I AM DAVID
ANNE HOLM

THE MILLION COPY
BEST SELLER

7 to 9

"David lay quite still in the darkness, listening to the men's low mutterings. 'You must get away tonight,' the man had told him. 'Stay awake so that you're ready just before the guard's changed.'" So begins this extraordinary, moving and constantly nail-biting story. David is a twelve-year-old boy who knows nothing about himself or how he has come to be inside a concentration camp. He also has no idea why he is then allowed to escape. Tramping across Southern Europe, cadging food and shelter as best he can, he is finally offered a home by a rich Italian family whose parents want to look after him after he saves their child from a fire. But he has to move on in order to discover who he is and what happened to him when he was too young to remember. He knows that the answer to this quest lies in Denmark, and when he gets there after travelling through Switzerland and Germany, things at last fall into place.

The author was herself Danish, and this book still remains a bestseller all over the world, with young readers continuing to write directly to David each year as if he was a real person. Although we never find out exactly where he comes from and how he ended up where he was, this deliberate vagueness helps turn David into a universal symbol for all displaced or abandoned young people – perhaps explaining why children from so many different countries have taken this story to their hearts. His adventures crossing Europe, however grim, also contain all the traditional appeal of the picaresque – a genre that focuses on journeys rather than arrivals. In such stories, characters normally meet a wide selection of other characters and also have numerous adventures before they get to their final destination. All this is true of David, who by perpetually moving on from one situation to another makes sure that neither he nor his readers ever get bogged down too long in any one place. The result is a narrative that is both highly readable and deeply moving, and one that continues to be as relevant today to the fate of so many children as it was for the displaced children of Europe during the immediate postwar years.

7 to 9

## Little House in the Big Woods

**Laura Ingalls Wilder** (author) **Garth Williams** (illustrator)

HarperCollins (hb & pb)

Life in a remote log cabin in the Wisconsin Woods over a hundred years ago was rarely easy. But there were consolations too, all of which are lovingly recorded in this famous book first published in 1932. Largely autobiographical, it describes how Laura and her sister Mary grew up learning to sow and harvest their own food, churn butter, smoke venison, recognize poisonous snakes and make their own entertainment. With the nearest town seven miles away, there is no thought of going to school. Instead there are bears and panthers to deal with, wild honey to be gathered and maple trees to

7 to 9

## The Complete Laura Ingalls Wilder Books

Little House in the Big Woods

Little House on the Prairie

Farmer Boy

On the Banks of Plum Creek

By the Shores of Silver Lake

The Long Winter

Little Town on the Prairie

These Happy Golden Years

7 to 9

tap. Best of all, there is Pa's singing along to his own fiddle on long evenings around the fire, with the children clapping hands and tapping their feet while Ma in the rocking chair gets on with some darning or sewing.

Written when the author was already over sixty, the prevailing mood of this first book in the series is one of nostalgia, with all the main characters shown in their best light and daily hardships played down in favour of a sense of continual optimism. Garth Williams's carefully researched, black-and-white drawings add to the overall impression of affectionate recall which has entranced readers for so many years. But, while the wealth of picturesque detail helps to create something of an idyll out of frontier life, the author also gives glimpses of how hard things could be when food supplies run low and the surrounding snow is particularly threatening. The result is a book that entertains and educates at the same time, written with charm and compassion by a natural storyteller. As the sequence of books which follow this one progresses, the girls gradually grow up, the family move further west and life becomes even more arduous.

## War Boy

**Michael Foreman** (author/illustrator)
Puffin (pb)

7 to 9

This illustrated autobiographical memoir is not a story as such, but it is nevertheless filled with memorable tales from a very special time in recent history. The artist-author grew up in a small Suffolk town during World War II, and this book records his recollections – from being bombed while lying in bed to having to walk home clad in a pair of bloomers after an unfortunate accident when visiting an aunt. Official government information is sometimes reproduced, such as a series of cigarette cards on how to cope with an incendiary bomb. The book finishes with pictures of dancing in the streets as the war is finally declared over. In between there are memories of other more ordinary moments from a country childhood, such as how to play games with different types of grass, or what happens when a large billy goat runs wild through the town.

Michael Foreman's mother ran a local shop during this time, and a number of the illustrations are set in her back parlour where soldiers, sailors and others regularly gather together in a warm and friendly atmosphere to play cards, drink tea and swap jokes, with all the adult characters pictured as if from a child's point of view. War Boy is a highly personal account, with stories, wry comments, odd details of history

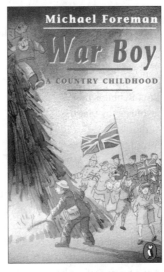

and local characters jumbled together very much in the way that memory itself tends to work. But it is also a memoir at pains to be accurate, with the general charm of the narrative coexisting with honest and unflinching descriptions of some of the tragedies that war brings about. This is a book to dip into over and over again, and it should also be popular with grandparents who may remember those times. A sequel, *After the War Was*

7 to 9

*Over*, continues the story up to the author's adolescence.

## When Hitler Stole Pink Rabbit

**Judith Kerr** (author/illustrator)

HarperCollins (hb & pb)

Pink Rabbit is the favourite toy that the author was forced to leave behind in Germany when she and her parents fled to Switzerland in 1933, one day before her father was due to be arrested by the Nazis. In this story, Judith Kerr describes herself as "Anna", but otherwise all the details are true. Because she is only nine years old at the time, Anna never realizes how great the danger facing Jewish people in Germany actually is, and this is a surprisingly happy account of such a difficult time; it was her parents who really suffered, knowing the terrible fate waiting them should they ever be returned to Germany. After Switzerland – where Anna becomes a big hit with the local boys – the family journeys to Paris, and finally makes it to Britain just before war breaks out. Had they

all stayed in France, they would almost certainly have
been killed.

Judith Kerr – who has also produced many books for
younger children – illustrates this novel herself. Anna
comes over as a sparky and irrepressible person in
whatever circumstances, so that readers can actually
enjoy her story despite the appalling dangers the family
had to face. But there are also glimpses of the suffering
others underwent during this time, made all the more
poignant by the contrast to Anna's own incredible good
fortune. Readers will find themselves asking how on
earth a child as charming as Anna (not to mention her
loving and amiable family) could ever have been seen
to pose a threat to the Nazis. There is no sane answer to
such a question, yet it is one that has to be asked and
responded to if present-day children are ever going to
make any sense of this dark period in European history.
The author does not attempt to give any such answers
herself. But by providing young readers with a picture
of a young Jewish girl so full of life within a family
determined to survive is in itself a gesture against
murderous tyranny.

Judith Kerr has written two sequels to this book; *The
Other Way Round* where Anna grows up in wartime
London, and *A Small Person Far Away* in which Anna
visits postwar Berlin.

## The Wool-Pack

**Cynthia Harnett** (author/illustrator)

Mammoth (pb)

Set in the Cotswolds in the year 1493, this is a stirring
story of skullduggery in the local wool trade. Its hero is
Nicholas Fetterlock, the son of a once-wealthy wool
merchant now fallen on hard times. A deal made with
some smooth-talking Italian moneylenders nearly leads
to disaster, but Nicholas finally thwarts a dastardly plot,
aided by his school friend turned servant Hal and an
eleven-year-old girl called Cecily to whom he is
betrothed. By the end of this story both he – and his
readers – have found out a great deal more about the
finer detail of wool trading in the Middle Ages. This
might sound dull, but the extraordinary level of
ingenuity shown by the medieval merchants when it
came to protecting their own profits while freezing out
everyone else has a fascination all of its own.
The author illustrates her text with meticulous
drawings on almost every other page. As she explains in
a short postscript, all these sketches are based on actual
houses or objects. Close attention to historical detail is
not in itself enough to make any book interesting to
children, but as part of a tense and suspenseful story
the overall effect is to make readers feel that for a short
time they have actually experienced what life in the
Middle Ages was actually like. Not everything is

pleasant: children will feel sorry for the bears that are baited at the fair and will be amazed at the way fathers once made their children bow down before them. But they should certainly enjoy reading about a time when children could leave school early, ride horses over wild countryside and then marvel at the sight of huge sailing ships at dock about to set off for undiscovered worlds.

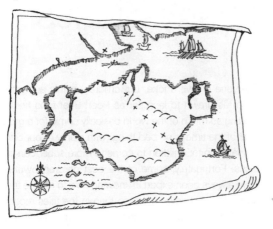

7 to 9

# Funny Stories

Everyone enjoys a joke, but children at this age often seem as drawn to laughter as Pooh Bear is to honey. Finding so much of the world basically comic for a great deal of the time is no bad thing, with plenty of opportunity later on for children to come to more sober conclusions. Fortunately, some of the best children's writers have always been expert in knowing how to amuse their audience, and never more so than in the titles recommended here. But being funny does not mean that writers cannot also make serious points at the same time, and these stories often contain strong moral messages. They are also consistently on the side of the young and the small, which often means attacking those adult characters who pursue a less sympathetic line. No wonder children usually adore such stories, thoroughly enjoying the chance of taking revenge in fiction against the sort of oppressive older characters so much more difficult to make a stand against in real life.

## Charlie and the Chocolate Factory

**Roald Dahl** (author) **Quentin Blake** (illustrator)
Viking (hb) Puffin Books (pb)

Charlie Bucket does not have a lot going for him at the beginning of this famous story. But when he finds a Golden Ticket that allows him a trip round a mysterious chocolate factory owned by Mr Willy Wonka, this changes his life. While the other four children on the tour come to sticky ends as a result of their various gross personal failings, Charlie does everything right and as a reward is finally given the factory as a present. He, his parents and grandparents can now live there for the rest of their lives, eating as much chocolate as they like in the process.

Roald Dahl himself had a soft spot for chocolate, always offering it to guests after meals and never forgetting the comfort it brought him when he was at boarding school. And indeed, there are other moments in this story where the author gives full rein to his childish side. He attacks characters he does not like, whether young or old, with all the rude and crude verbal energy normally heard in the playground. In this book, the junior victims who particularly irritate him

are the greedy Augustus Gloop, the hopelessly spoilt Veruca Salt, the perpetually gum-chewing Violet Beauregarde and Mike Teavee, "who does nothing but watch television". Their violent ends have sometimes upset adult critics, but child readers rarely have such scruples, recognising Dahl as one of their own when it comes to over-the-top humour at the expense of unpopular characters.

Dahl was a highly skilled writer, developing over the years an easy, colloquial style excellent for communicating directly with children. This story in particular crackles with energy, sometimes breaking out into verse that rattles along with equal conviction. Dialogue is always rapid, littered with the exclamation marks, capital letters and the occasional made-up words so characteristic of this writer when working at full throttle. Having first tried out this tale on his own children – who thoroughly enjoyed it – Dahl refused to allow worries about possible bad taste or insensitivity get in the way of a really good story. Child readers have in their turn rewarded Dahl by regularly voting his books their favourites, not just during his own lifetime but well after his death as well.

## The Gizmo

**Paul Jennings** (author) **Keith McEwan** (illustrator)

Puffin (pb)

Stephen is persuaded by his undesirable friend Floggit to steal something from a market stall run by a small man with strange eyes. Snatching up an electric gizmo shaped like a ball with little coloured windows, the boy hurtles away with it, only to feel instant remorse. After deciding to go back and make amends, he finds that the stall and its odd owner has now disappeared. But when he tries to throw away the gizmo, it keeps returning – just like a guilty conscience. To make matters worse it then starts to hum, and whenever this happens Stephen's clothes are immediately exchanged with those of whoever is nearest to him. This way he ends up first dressed in a tramp's outfit, then a wedding dress and lastly a bikini. Finally he loses the gizmo to the unpleasant Floggit, who is made to suffer even greater embarrassment. Now thoroughly relieved, Stephen vows never to steal again.

Brilliantly illustrated by Keith McEwan, this cautionary tale makes a serious point without ever

seeming to preach. Any story involving magic gizmos, losing one's clothes and looking stupid is bound to be fun, but behind this there is never any doubt that Stephen knows he has done something wrong and would do anything to put it right. Stealing from shops is an experience that more than a few children try out for themselves at some time, and they will also know about others their own age who have occasionally done the same. This story, as well as providing lots of amusement, also reminds young readers of the guilt that can follow such dishonesty; reading it with a child could also lead to some quite interesting and useful conversations long after the book is finished.

## The Hundred-Mile-An-Hour Dog

**Jeremy Strong** (author) **Nick Sharratt** (illustrator)
Puffin (pb)

This story is about Streaker – not so much a dog as "a rocket on four legs with a woof attached". Trevor gets the job of walking her in the holidays, and despite his ingenuity Streaker regularly proves too much for him. All the possible solutions to the dog's boundless energy that he comes up with not only fail to deliver but also get Trevor into constant trouble with Sergeant Smugg, an unpopular local policeman with an even nastier son named Charlie. But with the help of best friend Tina, the miraculous does eventually happen, and Streaker finally does what she is told.

This engaging story was voted winner of the Children's Book Award in 1997, and Jeremy Strong is certainly a wonderful writer. The events he describes are exaggerated but never too much so, and his language always keeps to the level of a young reader. There is also an element of truth behind much of his humour. So many pets in children's books come over as unbelievably well behaved and intelligent. Describing a dog who is neither provides a welcome breath of fresh air; making her loveable at the same time is one more example of the author's skill.

## Little Wolf's Book of Badness
**Ian Whybrow** (author) **Tony Ross** (illustrator)
HarperCollins (hb & pb)

Little Wolf is sent away to Cunning College for Brute

Beasts, which is run by his Uncle Bigbad, and is not allowed to return home until he has learned the famous Nine Rules of Badness. This book is made up of letters sent back to his mother and father, both anxious to make their own little wolf quite as bad as all other storybook wolves. But however hard he tries, Little Wolf's essential good nature always comes out on top. When he meets a troop of boy scouts, the temptation to do something good and constructive is just too much for him. How he finally ends up satisfying everyone – except his mean uncle, that is – provides a climax well worth waiting for.

Amusingly illustrated by Tony Ross, these apparently artless letters from Little Wolf in fact disguise a narrative where young readers are constantly having to read between the lines to make sense of what is really going on. At one stage, for example, it becomes clear that Uncle Bigbad is also the wolf in the story of Red Riding Hood. Little Wolf's boasting in letters home of

his own progress towards achieving a state of full
wickedness also ring increasingly hollow, while his
uncle gradually emerges as little more than a lying old
hypocrite. Although young readers are not told any of
this directly, they will soon learn to deconstruct the real
from the apparent. Solving this type of intellectual
puzzle could sound like hard work, but the author
writes with such wit and charm that every page is a
delight. Other stories in the series include *Little Wolf,
Forest Detective, Little Wolf's Diary of Daring Deeds* and
*Little Wolf's Haunted Hall for Small Horrors*.

## Vlad the Drac

**Ann Jungman** (author) **George Thompson** (illustrator)
HarperCollins (pb)

On a family holiday in Romania, Paul and Judy
discover a baby vampire whom they smuggle back to
Britain. Naming him after his remote ancestor Vlad the
Impaler, the two children hide him in a bedroom chest-
of-drawers on their return home. They can do this
because Vlad himself, as the world's only vegetarian
vampire, is never any real threat. His various antics,
however, can still be something of a nuisance, not least
when he gets drunk on sherry and pretends to have
eaten the milkman. Yet at heart he is all bark and no
bite; a cross between a playful younger child and a

favourite pet. Eventually the children's parents are in on the secret too, and Vlad is returned to his native country. Despite being proud to the very last, he also remains continually dependent on the children to help him out of the various difficulties he's always getting into.

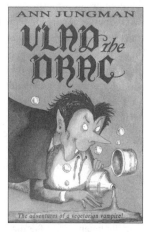

ANN JUNGMAN

VLAD the DRAC

The adventures of a vegetarian vampire!

Vlad himself is one more version of the fantasy companion that children like imagining as well as reading about at this age. He is by no means an ideal friend, but in a curious way this makes him more appealing since the two children end up having to behave towards him like parents. The idea rather than the actual practice of looking after others always has its attractions for the young, giving them a chance to try out in the imagination those parental skills that they are going to need in later life. But while any real description of what it is like to look after someone else for years on end would be too much at this age, stories of life with a fantasy child such as Vlad are a different matter. Funny, unpredictable, playful and defiant, he is always excellent company both in this story and in its various sequels. Illustrated by George Thompson in scratchy, atmospheric black-and-white drawings, these stories are excellent for young readers, particularly those already curious about the world of monsters and vampires but not quite ready as yet to take on the scarier examples of this genre.

## More of Vlad the Drac

Vlad the Drac Down Under

Vlad the Drac Superstar

Vlad the Drac Goes Travelling

Vlad the Drac Returns

## The William Stories

**Richmal Crompton** (author) **Thomas Henry** (illustrator)
Macmillan (hb & pb)

William Brown is a tough and permanently unruly eleven-year-old living in a village, surrounded by countryside, somewhere in the south of England. First published in a magazine in 1922, the stories about him were initially directed at an adult audience, which explains their occasionally elaborate vocabulary and topical social satire. But child readers quickly rallied to someone who behaves so badly yet who never gets seriously punished or reprimanded. William, along

with his dog Jumble and his gang of friends (known as the Outlaws), is generally shown being as naughty as it's possible to be, without ever feeling a twinge of guilt.

William lives at home with his distracted mother, a darkly suspicious father and two older siblings, John and Ethel, who look on him with unconcealed loathing. The Brown household is the epitome of middle-class gentility within which William is a total aberration. Such a scenario could be treated as the stuff of domestic tragedy were it not for the way that the author always looks on the entire family as an extended joke. Visiting aunts, uncles or other dignitaries also get short shrift from William – unless any are of the very rare breed who actually like him and the Outlaws. Outside the home, there are always plenty more pompous adults to deflate, plus occasional tramps or burglars – who usually manage to employ William and his friends for their own purposes. There are times when William does want to do his best, however regularly he ends up making everything much worse. He also has an enquiring mind, with many pages given over to his efforts to understand various adult intellectual challenges invariably far beyond his grasp.

Richmal Crompton had a keen sense of humour, and the jokes in these stories are usually excellent. She also had the benefit of the black-and-white illustrations provided over the years by Thomas Henry, who was expert in capturing the gently subversive humour of these stories. Subsequent illustrations have sometimes tried to bring William up-to-date by abandoning the school cap, askew collar and tie and knee-length socks that were part of his regular image for so many years. But those who want the full flavour of this great figure should seek out editions that still keep to the original format. For sheer laughter, there has never been anyone to beat William, and most of the 38 books of stories about him have lasted remarkably well into an era when cooks, gardeners and parlour maids now seem extremely dated.

7 to 9

# Poetry

Poetry can still be popular at this age, particularly when it is either comic or concentrates on telling a good story. But children are also now capable of appreciating poems that deal with some of the emotions they recognise from their own lives. Many such poems describe those special feelings that children treasure, from an appreciation of the beauty of nature to particular moments of intimacy or joy, while other poems address some of the darker, sadder emotions. What a good poet needs when writing for young children is the ability to communicate quickly and directly with their readers. Some adults may enjoy puzzling over more obscure poetry, but children at this age will generally have less patience with anything they cannot understand fairly speedily. Unless, of course, they know that they are reading nonsense which, while it is not meant to be understood, can still be enormous fun.

# Balloon Lagoon
# and the Magic Islands of Poetry

**Adrian Mitchell** (author) **Tony Ross** (illustrator)
Orchard (hb & pb)

To call Adrian Mitchell's poems unpredictable would be
a serious understatement. Although he writes about
familiar topics like children, animals and friends, each
poem moves from one idea to another in a way that
remains constantly surprising. The title poem gives
some idea of what is to follow: "Happy, sad,

ragamuffin, / Spooky and daft – / You'll meet them all /
On my poetry raft. / Dancing in the spotlight / Of a
Musical Moon / On the wobbly waters / of Balloon
Lagoon."

  Expressly forbidden by the author from being used in
"any examination or test whatsoever", what follows is a
series of wild and wacky ideas that gather strength as
they develop. Take, for example, "Nothingmas Day".
This describes an imaginary time when children are

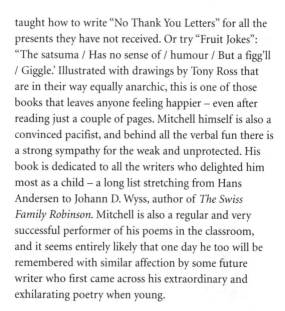

taught how to write "No Thank You Letters" for all the presents they have not received. Or try "Fruit Jokes": "The satsuma / Has no sense of / humour / But a figg'll / Giggle.' Illustrated with drawings by Tony Ross that are in their way equally anarchic, this is one of those books that leaves anyone feeling happier – even after reading just a couple of pages. Mitchell himself is also a convinced pacifist, and behind all the verbal fun there is a strong sympathy for the weak and unprotected. His book is dedicated to all the writers who delighted him most as a child – a long list stretching from Hans Andersen to Johann D. Wyss, author of *The Swiss Family Robinson*. Mitchell is also a regular and very successful performer of his poems in the classroom, and it seems entirely likely that one day he too will be remembered with similar affection by some future writer who first came across his extraordinary and exhilarating poetry when young.

## Collected Poems for Children
**Gareth Owen** (author)
Macmillan (hb & pb)

This collection is made up from three previously published books: *Salford Road*, *Song of the City* and *My Granny is a Sumo Wrestler*. The poet wrote the first volume in the 1960s but only found a publisher in

1979. This is a measure of how far poetry for children has come in the last thirty years, transforming itself from what was once seen as very much a minority taste into the mass genre that exists today. Owen himself has always been one of the most popular poets for children, and this collection soon explains why. Drawing on strongly autobiographical memories from his own childhood, his often comic narratives manage to bring all the confusion, fantasy and sense of adventure associated with childhood back to vivid poetic life.

This is writing that is always immediately accessible to children, concentrating on the common events known, enjoyed and sometimes dreaded by the young. Visits to the dentist, fights in the playground, puzzles over old photographs and talking with friends all find their way into this book, very often in poems written to a regular, rhyming verse form. Other poems take a more inventive view of rhyme, as in "We keep suggesting games to play / Like Monopoly / But you need a day / If you want to play / It properly." The tone is often jaunty, even in the face of personal disaster, as in the poem "Dear Examiner". This begins with some quietly desperate, mock-appreciative lines: "Thank you so much for your questions / I've read them all carefully through / But there isn't a single one of them / That I know the answer to." At other moments, the darker side of childhood is described less forgivingly, as in "Arthur the Fat Boy", which describes the way a former

7 to 9

classroom victim at last manages to get the better of his chief tormentors. Although mostly told as if by boys, there are poems where girls appear centre-stage too, playing long imaginary games during playtime or making and breaking various friendships in quick succession. There are no illustrations in this book, but these are not really necessary for a poet who is so adept in creating such instant and compelling images in his own verse.

## Let Me Touch the Sky

**Valerie Bloom** (author) **Kathy Lucas** (illustrator)

Macmillan (hb & pb)

7 to 9

Valerie Bloom was born in Jamaica but later studied in Britain. Her poems reflect both parts of her background, and although some are clearly written for performance they also read equally well. Many are about nature and its animals, as in "The hyena has neither charm nor wit. / Beauty and courage? He hasn't a bit, / In the animal world he has no clout, / So I don't know what he's laughing about." Others are written in Jamaican dialect, and although a glossary has been added at the back of this book the meaning is usually quite clear. Most children, for example, can fairly quickly get to understand language like "Barry madda tell ' im / But Barry wouldn' hear, / Barry fada warn ' 'im / But Barry didn' care. 'Don' go ova dere, bwoy, / Don' go ova dere.'

Other titles range from "Christmas Eve" to "Football Blues" – another poem written with vitality and considerable wit about the type of match every home supporter most dreads. Words that are not immediately clear nearly always come into focus once spoken. If this means that these poems often end up being read aloud this is no bad thing, since this is always a good way of discovering some of a poem's previously hidden riches. Valerie Bloom has written other poetry collections for children, but this one – pleasantly if sparingly illustrated with fine drawings by Kathy Lucas – is particularly worth looking out for.

## Mind Your Own Business
**Michael Rosen** (author) **Quentin Blake** (illustrator)
Scholastic (pb)

First published in 1974, this collection marked a complete break with the kind of poetry for children that existed up to that time. Written in unrhymed verse using the cadences of everyday speech, the poems themselves could at first sight be mistaken for chunks of dialogue. It is only on reading and re-reading them that the care with which each word is chosen finally becomes evident. Avoiding rhyme and metre in favour of the immediacy of everyday phrases, the poems work because they are also extremely funny and perceptive, describing feelings and situations that children will recognize from their own lives.

Most of the situations in these poems are drawn from the normal hurly-burly of family life when children constantly argue with parents attempting to reason or simply lay down the law. Both voices can be heard in one typical untitled poem that starts "If you don't put your shoes on before I count fifteen then we won't go to the woods to climb the chestnut". After that the adult voice starts counting, continually interrupted by various excuses from the child performing this simple task as slowly as possible. In these conditions, the adult in the poem finds themselves stretching out the penultimate number fourteen to a last agonized figure of "fourteen and fifteen sixteeeenths" before both shoes are finally on. Other poems discuss ordinary urban sights, big family occasions like weddings, games of pretend and the problems of sharing a bedroom with an exuberant brother. Quentin Blake, who provides the illustrations, catches exactly the right note of high spirits leading to occasional mayhem, and altogether

7 to 9

the book offers a perfect match of artist and writer. A prolific writer and classroom entertainer ever since this book first appeared, Rosen has gone on to publish many other poetry books for children. Adult readers may sometimes wonder whether his poems can actually be defined as poetry, but young readers are hardly going to worry. For children, the poet seems to be describing them, their families and their friends as if he actually knows them personally. The language he uses may look ordinary enough, but various cunningly throwaway phrases linger in the mind long afterwards – the essence of what poetry for children should be all about.

## The Poet Cat

**Grace Nichols** (author) **Bee Willey** (illustrator)
Bloomsbury (hb & pb)

These linked short poems trace the life of a cat from the moment when she first arrives to the time when she has become an inseparable part of the family. Different poems describe finding her a name and then the longer process of coming to terms with all the different facets of a pet who can be both a small tiger and a soft, affectionate presence. The writing throughout is simple, clear but never facile. Pleasantly illustrated with line drawings by Bee Willey, this is a book that will appeal

7 to 9

to cat lovers as well as to more neutral observers.

Grace Nichols can write the most ingenious rhyming verse, as in the last three lines of the poem "Attitude Problem": "That's what you get for gratitude, / when

you give a cat too much latitude – / a haughty heap of cattitude." At other times she offers only half-rhymes or no rhymes at all: "Overlooking the garden / as if she's a warden, treading on the daisies / without saying pardon." Children themselves seem naturally drawn to rhyme when young, but it does them good to realize early on that poets can sometimes have very different ways of producing their effects. This collection in fact contains everything from ordered, orthodox poetry to blank verse, all bound together by the common theme of the family cat. Some poems look back to the ancient Egyptian history of these animals, while others describe strictly contemporary events like the nuisance of cats singing at night. Not that the cats themselves see it quite like that, of course: "It's heart-rending, / their opposition, / to our musical compositions, / our varied renditions." Dedicated to the family cat and to the daughter who asked some of the questions that later turn up in the poems, this collection is original, amusing and intriguing. Other poetry collections by Grace Nichols have been published, and she has written a number of stories for children. With her husband John Agard, another gifted poet who writes for children, she has also collected nursery rhymes from their native Guyana as well as composing some new ones themselves.

## Sky in the Pie

**Roger McGough** (author) **Satoshi Kitamura** (illustrator)
Puffin (pb)

Roger McGough has always been fascinated by the English language itself, once declaring that "if you look after the words, the poems look after themselves." And in this anthology, his astonishing wordplay sometimes gets close to the genius of Lewis Carroll, particularly in examples like this: "Whalemeat again / (Don' t know where? / Don' t know when / But I know) / Whalemeat again / (some sunny day)." Other verses take their cue from common phrases such as "harum scarum" or "in cahoots", using their hidden poetic potential to weave a string of linked fantasies. In another poem, the

7 to 9

well-worn parental phrase "Time for bed" is turned into a person who is also a miserable spoilsport.

The subjects for these ingenious poems are often those close to a child's heart. On the topic of friends, for example, McGough writes "There's good mates and bad mates / 'sorry to keep you waiting' mates / Cheap skates and wet mates / The ones you end up hating mates." The poet also writes about his own loathing of violence in terms that underline its pointlessness: "My father beats me up / Just like his father did / And grandad he was beaten / by greatgrandad as a kid." There is throughout constant sympathy for children, especially when they are feeling small and vulnerable. The result is a collection that manages to be hilarious, stimulating, wildly inventive and very moving by turns. A series of excellent black-

and-white drawings by the distinguished illustrator Satoshi Kitamura translate the ideas in the poems into a visual language rich in puns and inferences of its own. If children – and adults – like this book, it would be worth looking out for some of the other thirty titles written by McGough, and particularly his *Helen Highwater*, also full of inspired wordplay.

## There's an Awful Lot of Weirdos in our Neighbourhood

**Colin McNaughton** (author/illustrator)

Walker (pb)

The tone of this anarchic, rumbustious collection is clear from its first poem: "The water's deep, / The sharks are thin, / The current's strong / So COME ON IN!" This teasing humour persists throughout the book, backed up by the author's own brand of uniquely over-the-top illustrations. These are always very much part of the joke, often giving an extra meaning to the poems they accompany. The junior footballer who writes about how many goals he has scored is cut down to size by a picture showing that he is in fact playing on his own in his back garden. The father who threatens his unruly children with a short, sharp shock sounds impressive enough but looks ridiculous, since he is pictured as less than half their size.

Various other giants crop up in these pages, sometimes hugging teddies and sucking at dummies

7 to 9

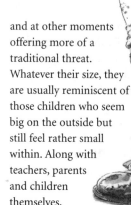

and at other moments offering more of a traditional threat. Whatever their size, they are usually reminiscent of those children who seem big on the outside but still feel rather small within. Along with teachers, parents and children themselves,

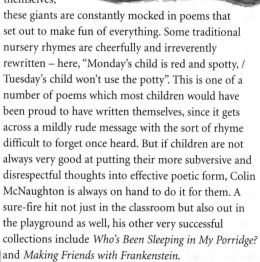

these giants are constantly mocked in poems that set out to make fun of everything. Some traditional nursery rhymes are cheerfully and irreverently rewritten – here, "Monday's child is red and spotty, / Tuesday's child won't use the potty". This is one of a number of poems which most children would have been proud to have written themselves, since it gets across a mildly rude message with the sort of rhyme difficult to forget once heard. But if children are not always very good at putting their more subversive and disrespectful thoughts into effective poetic form, Colin McNaughton is always on hand to do it for them. A sure-fire hit not just in the classroom but also out in the playground as well, his other very successful collections include *Who's Been Sleeping in My Porridge?* and *Making Friends with Frankenstein*.

7 to 9

# Pre-teens

## 9 to 11

# Pre-
# teens

## 9 to 11

Within this age group children now tend to choose the stories they want to read more or less for themselves. Some of the books recommended are aimed at readers aged over eleven, but there is nothing wrong with that, given that children often like to read about characters who are older than themselves involved in situations yet to be encountered in their own lives. Many of the stories are also more mature in other ways. The characters within them may not always fit easily into "good" or "bad" categories, just as people often do not in real life. At the same time, what happens in a plot may not always be totally clear – again, as in life itself. But readers of this age are now ready for stories that make them think at a deeper level as well as offering rich entertainment. Some darker topics, usually avoided in books for younger readers, also make their way into a number of these stories. There was a time when many adults tried to keep children away from books thought unsuitable for them, but there is less anxiety on this score now, given that so many children watch news bulletins, soap operas and other programmes which also frequently contain hard-hitting and explicit material.

But there are no stories in the following pages that set out to shock for shock's sake. Although the writers included here discuss almost every possible topic, they all do so responsibly and thoughtfully. They also continue to include many traditional themes, topics and characters in their stories, that still appeal directly to modern children just as they always have done. The young often want to read about the young, for example, and there are hundreds of child characters to choose from in the books that follow, ranging from the nice to the truly horrible. Children also still like reading stories containing animal characters, however human such characters often seem to be. Like all the other books selected here, some of these stories are basically serious, others are very funny, and many manage to be both at the same time.

Young readers may also around now start turning to

books principally aimed at adult readers. But this does not mean that they have given up on children's books for good. Some adult novels have always attracted young readers, just as the best writing for children has often had much to offer all ages. Towards the end of the nineteenth century, for example, adult readers were often very happy to read some of the most celebrated children's books of their times. Such crossing over became less fashionable later on, but today shows signs of reviving once again. This should not surprise anyone acquainted with the work of the best contemporary children's authors who have so much to offer not just young readers but very often much older ones as well.

9 to 11

# Classics

The old-fashioned attitudes and language that can be found within books written for children long ago sometimes strike young readers as rather comic. But this type of reaction is usually forgotten when such apparent quaintness is incorporated into the kind of thrilling storytelling that has so enthralled previous generations of readers. Several of the most gripping tales in this section concentrate on characters trying to cope on their own in difficult situations, and the particular type of courage and imagination that is required in order for them to win through. Others take up favourite daydreams and then show how badly these might turn out once translated into fictional reality. In all of them, young characters are depicted not as super-heroes but more as ordinary types made extraordinary because of the extremity of the adventures they have. Such characters are often shown to have faults as well as virtues, but this type of honesty also tends to make them that much more believable. It is precicely this veracity which has enabled a handful of classic titles to survive – out of the thousands written – and be taken into the hearts of successive generations with such enthusiasm.

## Anne of Green Gables
**L.M. Montgomery** (author)
Everyman (hb) Puffin (pb)

Anne is an eleven-year-old orphan who is offered a home by Matthew and Marilla Cuthbert, an elderly brother and sister living in a remote Canadian farm around the beginning of the twentieth century. This was never meant to happen, since the two were actually looking for a boy to help out at Green Gables farm. But once the shy, tongue-tied Matthew meets her, he can't find the words to

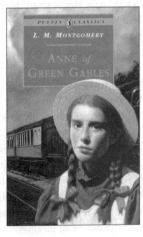

**9 to 11**

tell the little girl she isn't wanted. Brother and sister soon take to the affectionate, talkative child who is forever living in one dream or another. School and a best friend follow, but there is trouble with local boy Gilbert Blythe who has the cheek to tease Anne about her red hair. Her attempts to dye it a different colour lead to disaster, but harmony is restored and Anne soon becomes a favourite with everyone.

Such is the popularity of *Anne of Green Gables* that several replicas of the farm now exist in Japan, and every year fans trek over to Prince Edward Island off the East Coast of Canada where the story is set. Stories about orphans who come good in their new families have always been popular with young readers. Most ordinary parents love their children as a matter of course, so the idea of often initially hostile guardians gradually being won over by sheer charm is a fascinating idea for children. But *Anne of Green Gables* is also a beautifully written story, looking back nostalgically to an idealized countryside existence.

None of the many sequels to this story are quite as good as the first one, though many children also enjoy *Anne of Avonlea* (the next story in line), which describes Anne's life as a young teacher on the island.

## Ballet Shoes

**Noel Streatfield** (author) **Ruth Gervis** (illustrator)

Puffin (pb)

This was one of the first stories about talented children working hard and finally mastering the particular skill they seem to have been born with. It's also one of the best. Subtitled "A story of three children on the stage", it introduces readers to Pauline, Petrova and Posy, all orphans adopted by a vague and often absent great-uncle. They live affectionately

**9 to 11**

together in London with the uncle's great-niece Sylvia, who never has much money but manages to get by. The children take lessons from other lodgers rather than go to school, but soon their interest turns to a nearby Children's Academy of Dancing and Stage Training. After intense competition, several disappointments and a couple of sharp lessons, Posy eventually turns into a ballet dancer, Pauline begins a career as a film actress while Petrova decides to take up flying.

The author spent ten years on the stage herself, and writes about the business of learning how to dance or act with a realism that has captivated and convinced readers ever since. Young characters like these who have a talent that finally enables them to compete on equal terms with adults have always been popular in storytelling for children. By virtue of their skills, such characters are seen to possess a type of high standing with others that children in real life can enjoy fantasizing about and aspiring to. Noel Streatfield always emphasizes the hard work and tough exercise regimes necessary to achieve any sort of stardom, so that young readers will feel that each character's final success has been well and truly earned. The author went on to produce many other "career" novels – notably White Boots, which stars a young skater – but *Ballet Shoes* is the story she will always be remembered by.

## The Box of Delights

**John Masefield** (author)

Mammoth (pb)

9 to 11

The subtitle of this story is "When the wolves were running", and run they do in the half-fantastical, half-realistic Britain found in this book, where so many unexpected events take place in quick succession. Kay Harker, the young male hero meets a certain Cole Hawlings, a travelling entertainer who also possesses a magic box that can transport people to the past. But Abner Brown, a villain disguised as a clergyman-headmaster, is determined to get his hands on it too. Kidnaps and escapes follow, with the forces of evil – backed up by a darkly funny witch and a grumbling rat – only just behind Kay as he desperately strives to keep out of their clutches. Abner Brown will have won if he manages to stop the Christmas service in the local cathedral, but although he manages to abduct all the clergymen involved, Kay and Cole Hawlings still have some tricks left up their sleeves.

The author brings some poetic twists to this story, with Kay able to use the magic box to his heart's content in order to change himself into different animals whether huge or tiny. This sort of magic can seem childish to readers in this age group, but when presented as vividly as it is here, it still carries all the satisfaction of imagining being able to do the impossible. *The Box of Delights* is a sequel to the same author's *The Midnight Folk*: first published in 1935, it remains his most appealing work for children and has been adapted for radio and as a very successful TV series.

## Heidi

**Johanna Spyri** (author) **Cecil Hall** (illustrator)
Puffin Books (pb)

Five-year-old Heidi, already an orphan, is taken away from her village home in Switzerland to live with a grandfather high in the surrounding Alps.

Nick-named Alm-Uncle, because the crude herdsman hut he lives in is situated on a peak named Alm, the old man is gradually won over by the little girl as is everyone else she meets. Heidi also befriends the blind grandmother of her great friend young Peter the goatherd, but her new life falls apart when she is forced to return to town life in order to be a companion to the crippled child of a rich family. Finally, to universal acclaim, she returns to the mountains she pines for. The story ends with Heidi and Peter helping the same crippled child to a full recovery in the course of teaching her to walk.

Written in 1881 and translated into English three years later, this story has stayed a favourite with children ever since, its popularity bolstered by various film or television adaptations. Its penchant for religious preaching may now seem old-fashioned, but the particular daydream that informs this story is eternal in its appeal to children. Heidi is a classic example of a child heroine who can do no wrong, with every adult who encounters her eventually testifying to her charm and goodness. Before such successes there are also some difficult Cinderella-type times to get through, particularly when she is staying with a family perpetually appalled by her ignorance of city life and its various artificial rules of etiquette. But such reverses only serve to make Heidi's final triumph all the sweeter.

Set in a thoroughly idealized picture of traditional

rustic living in the Alps, this story is arguably the most successful, feel-good fantasy ever written for children. Likely to be unused to perpetual praise and appreciation in their own lives, young readers can instead relish the opportunity offered here to imagine themselves in the position of a girl who always eventually gets her way while charming every adult she comes into contact with.

## The Jungle Book
**Rudyard Kipling** (author)
Everyman (hb) Penguin (pb)

Out hunting in the Indian jungle one night, Father Wolf comes across Mowgli, an abandoned baby – but one who can just walk and has enough spirit to laugh in his face. He decides to take this "man-cub" home to be looked after by Mother Wolf, but this does not please Shere Khan, a ferocious tiger. He thinks that the baby is his rightful quarry, and remains a dangerous enemy while Mowgli grows up in the jungle, learning all the animal ways and in particular whom to trust. These lessons are often hard-won, with Kaa the python and the unruly monkeys of the Bandar-Log both nearly leading to Mowgli's death. But he scrapes by, and there is never a dull moment before he finally leaves the jungle and his beloved wolf pack for his own kind.

Although Walt Disney made an enjoyable film with the same title, it has none of the tense excitement and vivid detail of this marvellous story.

Children have always had a special sympathy for animals, seeing them as natural allies against the adult rules that often dominate their own lives. Left to their own devices children, like animals, adore roaming at will, something that Baden-Powell recognized when he founded his Scout movement, looking to *The Jungle Book* for the titles of the various pack leaders. This was an inspired choice, given that hundreds of thousands of children since have been particularly attracted by the idea of Mowgli and his jungle existence. As a hero he has all the advantages of being human (running on two legs and with the power of speech) as well as the privilege of being treated as a wild animal (no school, lots of physical activity and hours of freedom). Kipling was one of the great storytellers of all time, and readers who enjoy *The Jungle Book* could also try his delightful *Just So Stories*, also set in India and involving once again a sympathetic look at the world of animals.

## Little Women
**Louisa M. Alcott** (author)
Everyman (hb) Penguin (pb)

This famous story describes the lives of the teenage

March sisters – Meg, Jo, Beth and Amy – who live in a pleasant American town in the middle of the nineteenth century. Father is away working as a chaplain in the Civil War, but mother (always referred to as "Marmee") is very much in charge. With little money to spare, much of the girls' time is spent in each other's company. At various times they put on a play, form a secret society, and pass hours just gossiping, particularly about the young and eligible Laurie, who has recently moved in next door with his rich grandfather and wishes to make friends. While Marmee is happy with this, her stern sense of duty also insists that her daughters make regular visits to the poor and sick. Two of the girls eventually go down with scarlet fever, at that time a very dangerous illness, and more drama follows, including an engagement for one daughter and a wonderful surprise for another.

First published in 1868, Little Women is one of the first family stories written for children, and provides an unforgettable picture of a time when domestic closeness provided hours of companionship for all those involved. Told very largely in dialogue, the author clearly loves her characters (based on her own family) but does not sentimentalize them. There are quarrels as well as reconciliations and endearing weaknesses as well as formidable strengths. Best of all, Jo's spirited refusal to accept current ideas about what a young woman should and should not be remains as moving and memorable as it must have seemed when the book first appeared and is perhaps one reason why it has remained a bestseller ever since. The saga of Jo March continues in *Little Men* and *Jo's Boys*.

## The Railway Children
**E. Nesbit** (author) **C.E. Brock** (illustrator)
Everyman (hb) Penguin (pb)

With father in prison on trumped-up charges, mother and the children are now facing poverty and have to leave their happy life in London in order to live in a small, run-down, rat-infested cottage in the country. Very much on their own, with the mother occupied in trying to secure her husband's release, the three children soon make friends with the locals, and particularly with Mr Perks the Station Master. Things do not always run smoothly – there are various misunderstandings, a near rail accident, and an attempt to do good that almost ends in disaster. But everything gets cleared up in the end, and the moment when the children and their father are reunited must be one of the most moving final pages in all children's fiction.

There is no mention of school anywhere in this story, with the children enjoying a comparatively carefree time. But they are also up against the fact of their own poverty, and the way they cope with this, eventually winning over a rich philanthropist to their side, illustrates the type of compensatory fantasy always popular with young readers. Nesbit is also a superb writer: funny, non-judgmental and always firmly on the side of her young characters. She has a natural feeling for what interests children and a highly developed skill at avoiding what bores them. She also wrote other family adventures in *Five Children and It* and produced two exciting time-travel yarns in *The Phoenix and the Carpet* and *The Story of the Amulet*.

## The Secret Garden
**Frances Hodgson Burnett** (author) **Robin Lawrie** (illustrator)
Everyman (hb) Puffin (pb)

**9 to 11**

Children's books do not usually start by introducing a really unpleasant young heroine, but this one is an exception. Mary is a spiteful, sulky and rude girl, sent away to live with her uncle after her parents died in India. She thinks she is the only child in his big lonely house on the Yorkshire moors until the night when she hears the noise of crying down a distant corridor. Going to explore, she meets Colin, also cross and complaining and (up to that moment) believed ill enough to have to stay permanently in bed. Gradually they make friends through their interest in an overgrown garden that has been hidden away for ten years. With the help of a local boy, the children set about cultivating this garden and in doing so turn into much nicer and fitter people. They also discover the sad reason why the garden has been shut away for so long.

9 to 11

Gardens have always been places where children can escape the rules that govern living in a house, and the idea of a secret garden has the extra appeal of further independence from interfering adults. In such a space, children can imagine to their heart's content, just as they do in this story except that here their fantasies finally come true. The idea of getting closer to nature is also popular with children, so long as it is not accompanied by too many attempts at education, although in this story it is the children who educate the adults – always a very satisfying idea for the young. If readers enjoy it, they could also try the same author's *A Little Princess*, another highly pleasurable story about children making good against the odds.

## Swallows and Amazons
**Arthur Ransome** (author/illustrator)
Jonathan Cape (hb) Red Fox (pb)

Four children are allowed to sail off to a little island in the Lake District on their own, leaving behind parents who are happy for them to stay away for as long as they like. Sitting around the campfire they have made for themselves, they are confronted by the sudden appearance of "a long arrow with a green feather stuck, quivering, among the embers". This is a declaration of war by two other children, also claiming the island as their own. It's not long before everyone decides to join forces, but just playing at battles can be exciting enough, especially when these involve dangerous nighttime sailing without lights. A real burglary followed by a false accusation raises other problems, but nothing can really get in the way of a perfect holiday where the children do just as they want – even if they have to work hard at all the things normally taken care of by adults.

This story is based on some real-life sailing adventures Ransome had with four Lake District children he got to know as friends. It was the first "holiday" story for children, where young characters are shown solving their own day-to-day problems without any help from grown-ups. The problems in question are never serious

ones, but they are still important enough to characters intent on proving that they really can survive on their own. This is a story that makes young readers think positively about themselves and their capacities, even if only in the imagination. Ransome wrote many other holiday adventure books, with *We Didn't Mean to Go to Sea* probably the most exciting since it's here, as the title implies, that things nearly do go very wrong for all concerned.

## More from Arthur Ransome

| | |
|---|---|
| Secret Water | Pigeon Post |
| Peter Duck | Missee Lee |
| Swallowdale | The Big Six |
| Winter Holiday | Great Northern? |
| Coot Club | |

## The Sword in the Stone
**T.H. White** (author) **Robert Shadbolt** (illustrator)
HarperCollins (pb)

In the days before King Arthur, Sir Ector lives in a castle with his two sons: Kay and his adopted younger brother, known as the Wart. It was the bossy and resentful Kay who first called him this disparaging name, since it rhymes with his real name, which is

"Art". When Kay loses his hawk in the forest one day, Wart as usual gets the blame and is sent back to find it. Instead he comes across a strange old man who turns out to be Merlyn the Magician. He becomes the boy's tutor, specializing in the sort of magic where they are both at times turned into fishes, badgers or snakes. This is not without danger; there are also encounters with the bullying giant Galapas and the sinister witch, Madame Mim. But the main mood of this magical book is good-humoured and affectionate.

This novel was the cornerstone for the four books the author wrote about King Arthur in a series called *The Once and Future King*. There is no serious attempt to re-create Arthurian times, and the author constantly amuses himself by employing numerous anachronisms. But the gentle irony and moments of slapstick comedy coexist with a passionate story about what it is like to feel underappreciated when young. The author places a great deal of emphasis on the value of a sustaining friendship with an older person through which it can finally become possible to build up some sort of self-esteem, and long before the climax of this wonderful story Wart is shown as having at last come out from the shadows to claim his full rights as a human being. Cinderella-type stories are always popular with children, and like so many other classics this novel appeals on several levels.

**9 to 11**

## The Once and Future King

| The Sword in the Stone | The Candle in the Wind |
| The Witch in the Wood | The Book of Merlyn |
| The Ill-Made Knight | |

## Treasure Island
**Robert Louis Stevenson** (author)
Everyman (hb) Penguin (pb)

This wonderful adventure story really has everything: a terrifying, blind would-be murderer who always finds his man; a villainous one-legged pirate who's all charm on the outside and wickedness within; buried treasure; a talkative parrot; mutiny at sea; a desert island and a mad castaway. All this is seen through the eyes of Jim Hawkins, an intrepid young lad who leaves the inn run by his mother for a seafaring life during which he narrowly misses death by inches. No wonder he is happy eventually to return home safely, even if it's with "the sharp voice of Captain Flint still ringing in my ears, 'Pieces of eight! Pieces of eight!'"

Stevenson wrote this story for his stepson after the two passed the time one quiet day sketching out a map of an imaginary island containing buried treasure. But although the story is packed with incident, children are also drawn to the outsize characters within it. Long John Silver is not entirely bad – at one stage he saves Jim's life – but he is certainly no angel either. Squire Trelawney and the Doctor Livesey, who finance the whole trip, are honourable men in themselves, yet their own greed nearly does for the entire party. Characters whose morals are at best ambiguous offer an interesting challenge to young readers used to easy simplifications in their fiction, and coming to terms with this sort of complexity can

9 to 11

be an important part of a child's growing understanding of real life. Several films have been made of this story, but the book itself is still as fresh as when it was first published over a hundred years ago.

## Treasure Island Illustrated

The rich cast of characters and exotic locations of *Treasure Island* present a wonderful opportunity to a gifted illustrator, and many of the finest have risen to the occasion – from **Edmund Dulac** to **Ralph Steadman**. Of the classic illustrated editions, perhaps the most celebrated is that of American **N.C. Wyeth**, whose full-page colour plates combine a muscular energy with a palpable air of mystery and menace. His version first appeared in 1911 and is currently published by Simon & Schuster. **Mervyn Peake**'s brilliant line drawings – for the hardback edition recommended above – also project an essentially dark vision of the book, concentrating on character rather than period detail. More recently **François Place** has produced a series of beautifully-observed watercolours that unfortunately are only available in a French translation of the novel. Of recent British editions, the one published by Pavilion Classics is the most individual: **Justin Todd**'s paintings have a bejewelled, hallucinatory quality with dramatically close-up viewpoints that intensify the immediacy of the scene depicted.

# Historical Stories

**9 to 11**

Whether history is a favourite subject or not, historical stories can make the past come alive in a way that history textbooks rarely do, and most young readers enjoy getting involved with a really well-told story set in the past.

Child characters within such fiction are often shown coming up against the kind of dangers which were relatively common when life was harsher and more risky than is the case in Britain now. Young readers may find themselves wondering how they would have managed in such conditions and historical fiction provides them with possible answers, whether the period of times chosen by their authors are ancient or comparatively

recent. But dwelling on the past does not necessarily mean that any story necessarily has to neglect the present, and some of these tales are also relevant to social issues – like poverty – which are unfortunately still a part of modern life. Other stories concentrate more on past pleasures and excitements, offering young readers the literary equivalent of a time-machine with which they can explore those aspects of history that particularly fascinate and intrigue them.

## Carrie's War
**Nina Bawden** (author) **Faith Jaques** (illustrator)
Orion (hb) Puffin (pb)

Carrie and her brother Nick have no choice – along with thousands of other city-dwelling British children in 1940, they must leave their parents behind and be evacuated to the countryside to escape the enemy bombing. They finally arrive in a small Welsh village to stay with Mr Evans, a local shopkeeper and something of a bully, and his timid, but much nicer, sister Auntie Lou. Things get easier when Carrie discovers the home, deep in the countryside, of Mr Evans's sister Dilys with whom he no longer speaks. Carrie and Nick visit the house every day where they also meet Hepzibah, a kindly housekeeper, and Albert Sandwich, another evacuated child. Between them they look after Mr

Johnny, a harmless adult with the mind of a child.
Things start falling apart when Dilys dies and Mr Evans
suspects that he is being swindled out of family money.

This story, both funny and sad, is so convincing that
reading it is like becoming an evacuated child oneself.
The conflict of loyalties Carrie experiences will also
seem real to young readers, most of whom will have
had some experience of trying to keep all parties happy
in a potentially explosive situation. Mr Evans starts off
as a small-town bully, but by the end Carrie comes to
recognize that he does have some right on his side after

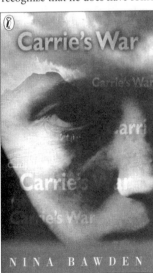

all. The moment
when a young
character realizes
that making moral
judgements of
others may not be
as easy as it
sometimes seems
occurs in all this
author's stories. It is
a lesson children
must eventually
learn for themselves,
but a novel such as
this can act as a first
step towards
understanding some

of the complexities of the adult world. But Nina Bawden also provides abundant excitement and suspense before ending her story on a reassuringly positive note. Among her many other excellent books for children, *The Peppermint Pig* and *Granny the Pag* are particularly successful.

## Coram Boy
**Jamila Gavin** (author)
Mammoth (pb)

9 to 11

Captain Thomas Coram was an actual eighteenth-century figure who set up the first orphanage for unwanted and abandoned children in London. *Coram Boy* tells of how unscrupulous characters would, for a fee, take the children of poor people (who were unable to look after them), promising to deliver them to Coram's Foundling Hospital. In reality, they often left them to die, taking no care of them at all on what might be an extremely long journey to London. One such brute is described in this darkly compelling novel, along with his son Meshak, who hates what his father is doing. Other main characters include Toby, saved from an African slave ship, and Alexander, thrown out of his home by his father because he wants to become a musician. Alexander later meets the great composer Handel (a major benefactor of the Hospital), but there are many twists and turns in this story before everything is resolved.

The author has written about India in her superb *The Wheel of Surya* and its two sequels, and in this novel she shows that she's equally at home with British history. Comparatively little children's fiction has been written about the more extreme conditions that some children experienced in the past, and the most shocking details in this story will come as a surprise to many. It is important, though, for young readers to know what life was like for children close to their own age given that legions of children across the world still experience similar hardships and danger. To this political message the author adds a personal one on the importance of always standing up for one's most precious beliefs, which is what Alexander has to do when he refuses to accept his father's plans for his future.

## The Diary of a Young Girl
**Anne Frank** (author)
Penguin (hb & pb)

This is the true story of Anne Frank who, in 1942, at the age of thirteen went into hiding with her family in the back of an Amsterdam warehouse. They were only just in time; shortly afterwards all Dutch Jews were rounded up by the Nazi occupiers and in most cases

9 to 11

sent to their death. Despite the fact that they seemed safe for the moment, life in the annexe was far from easy; crammed into a small space were Anne's own parents, the Van Daan family and a middle-aged dentist – all forbidden from making any noise whatsoever during the working day. Although fed by loyal friends outside, there was still barely enough food at a time when everyone in Holland was going short.

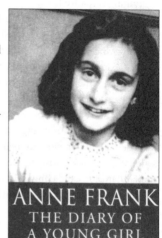

ANNE FRANK
THE DIARY OF
A YOUNG GIRL
NEW TRANSLATION
EDITED BY OTTO H. FRANK AND MIRJAM PRESSLER
THE DEFINITIVE EDITION

For the next two years Anne kept a detailed diary, describing not just the strange shut-away life she was leading but also her own feelings as she lives from day to day. She describes with honesty her increasing irritation with her mother, as well as her growing feeling of tenderness for Peter van Daan, a boy three years older than Anne and also going through some quite normal conflicts with his own family.

The diary ends abruptly at the moment when the

entire group is betrayed by an informer, and Anne eventually dies in a concentration camp three months short of her sixteenth birthday. Her extraordinary spirit lives on in this book, one of the most important to be published since World War II. Anne herself was a born writer: her descriptions of going through adolescence in highly artificial and cramped surroundings still have a truthfulness about them that appeals particularly to younger readers at the same stage of life themselves. Anne is also no angel – her opinions on others can be waspish as well as very funny – but her courage, patience and ultimate tolerance of others is as memorable as it is profoundly moving.

## The Eagle of the Ninth
**Rosemary Sutcliff** (author) **Tony Karpinski** (illustrator)
Penguin (pb)

In 117AD the Ninth Roman Legion was told to put down a rebellion in Scotland. Four thousand men marched off north from York, but were never heard of again. Centuries later Rosemary Sutcliff set out to solve this mystery in one of her best stories. She tells a tale of bad leadership and the gradual loss of men through raids, ambushes and finally desertion before the remaining soldiers of the legion are defeated and killed in a heroic last stand. But Marcus Aquila, son of the

**9 to 11**

slain Commander, sets out to clear his father's name of accusations of cowardice. His travels in disguise take him deep into British territory, where he learns to respect the native people he meets who are fighting for their country against invaders from outside. More battles and some rough sessions with gladiators follow, concluding with a climax which still sees Rome remaining in charge of Britain, but only just.

Rosemary Sutcliff wrote many other stories about the Roman occupation, ending with *The Lantern Bearers*, which describes the problems caused when the Romans suddenly decided to quit Britain altogether. Although she has a marked talent for evoking exciting set-pieces such as battles, she's also expert in describing the various psychological states of her younger characters, particularly in relation to their

own parents. In this way, she makes ancient history seem like an essentially personal process, with dates, and other dry matter always firmly in the background. Often in pain from a crippling disease that kept her at home for most of her life, she also had particular sympathy for outsiders in her fiction. Child readers looking for heroics in her novels will find them – but they will also find characters who sometimes have a tough time and find it difficult to manage. In all her books Rosemary Sutcliff lent history the type of human face still too often absent from classroom lessons.

## Fire, Bed and Bone
**Henrietta Branford** (author)
Walker (hb & pb)

Fourteenth-century Britain was a particularly hard time for everyone, so it was hardly surprising that in 1381 the peasants decided to revolt against cruel masters who asked for much but gave little in return. What happened both before and after the Peasants' Revolt is related in this story by a large hunting dog, witness to everything that has happened around her. The author, brought up in the New Forest, already knew about dogs from a father and grandfather who were both keen hunters. But later she turned vegetarian, and the compassion she came to feel for all suffering animals – as well as for humans – is evident in this exciting story. There are some tough moments, involving murder, torture, and terrible injustice, but there is never any risk of boredom as events gallop from one climax to another. The old dog is too clever for those out to get her as well as for her, but her gentle master is finally thrown into prison and executed for his beliefs about equality. She finishes her story surrounded by her former puppies and safely back once again with a fire to warm her, a bed for shelter and a bone for food.

History is often told to children through the lives of great men or women who, though often admirable in themselves, are still somewhat remote from the life of an ordinary eleven-year-old. By making a dog the chief witness to history, all the different political, economic aspects of this story are brought to a level that is easily understood by all. The Peasants' Revolt is also an event where children's sympathies can easily be raised on behalf of the poor and dispossessed. Bringing a favourite pet to this situation makes a favourable reader reaction even more likely, and this must be one of the most child-friendly history stories yet written for the young. The same author's *White Wolf*, set in Canada and dedicated to the wolves that still remain there, is also highly recommended.

## Going Back

**Penelope Lively** (author)

Penguin (pb)

Like *Carrie's War*, this story is set in the country during

World War II, but this time Jane and Edward are staying in their family's old house, which possesses a huge and fascinating garden. With their mother dead and their father often away on war business, the children make friends with some land girls and also with a man called Mike, who works on the land because he does not agree with the idea of fighting and killing. The children's father disapproves of this friendship, nor does he get on well with his son and daughter when he returns home. And when Edward finally runs away from the boarding school he quickly comes to loathe, there is no one left to turn to but Mike, now living somewhere else. By this time Mike has decided he will join the army after all, with the children coming to realize that in life there are always going to be hard choices to make.

This is not a long story, but it is wise, often funny, and full of detail from a time when children – along with everyone else – were living very upside-down lives. For some, it was also a time of moral confusion; in this particular case for Mike, who begins the war as a pacifist but ends up enlisting. Although he is a far more sympathetic character than the children's awkward and insensitive father, some readers may conclude that in this particular case it is the father who made the right choice to begin with. Others may come to a different conclusion – but one sign of a stimulating novel is that it can be read in a number of ways. The author is also

**9 to 11**

fascinated by the process of memory itself. Why do we remember some details from the past but not others? Do we always remember some of the strong emotions we once held, or do they eventually fade away? What, for example, might young readers still remember one day about a novel such as this one? And why does the author choose to end her narrative with the news that Edward himself later dies as a soldier? Because there are no firm answers to these questions child readers will have to make up their own minds, so ensuring that they continue to think about the book long after they have actually finished it.

## Goodnight Mister Tom

**Michelle Magorian** (author)
Penguin (pb)

This is another book about wartime evacuation, but in this one young Willie Beech leaves behind a mother who not only beats him but who is a religious maniac. He stays with old Tom Oakley, who lives with his dog in a dark but comfortable cottage. Willie has been so neglected that, incredibly, he believes that beds are something you lie under rather than on top – but gradually Tom brings him round, teaching him to read and giving him the affection he has previously lacked. But then Willie is summoned back home to his mother, who by now has gone quite mad. The beatings start again, and Willie ends up tied to a copper pipe in a locked room, abandoned and starving. It is here that Tom finds him, having come up to London sensing that something had gone very wrong. Willie goes to hospital and shortly after is to be sent into care, but when Tom hears about this he steals him away back to the village where he has been so happy.

This heartwarming story provides another slant on the evacuation of children during World War II. Although this is an event that happened over sixty years ago, it is still a topic that often interests young readers today. But while other stories set in the evacuation stress a child's homesickness, in this book Willie is only too glad of the change. Old Tom also benefits from this situation, and though he and Willie live in comparative poverty, the feeling is that they are both having a much richer time together than would be true if they were apart. There is a rather romantic view of life in the countryside in this story, and it's unlikely that many children would so happily renounce town for village life. But there is much to think about and enjoy in a novel that is highly reminiscent of George Eliot's *Silas Marner*, which also describes an old man rejuvenated by the unexpected experience of bringing up a small child.

9 to 11

## The Kin
**Peter Dickinson** (author) **Ian Andrews** (illustrator)
Macmillan (hb & pb)

*The Kin* is a prehistoric race different from any other because its members have at last learned how to communicate through language. Their story starts when a murderous tribe drives them from the land they have occupied for many generations. Setting out for new territory, they encounter a series of appalling dangers including volcanic eruptions, earthquakes and floods. There are also huge crocodiles and man-eating lions to contend with, but the greatest threat comes from various enemy groupings who have yet to evolve to the same level of the Kin. Divided into four parts, each representing the viewpoint of four different children, Suth, Noli, Ko and Mana, *The Kin* is a compelling story describing how early humans might have evolved as a race. Readers can see the way that certain skills gradually develop and get passed on until finally something like society itself becomes organized. But there is never any certainty that things will turn out well, since the final battle that takes place is within the Kin itself. Are its members going to go forward, or will they stay forever trapped in ancient hatreds?

Peter Dickinson is an ambitious writer, always eager to challenge young readers intellectually while also telling them an excellent story. His descriptions of how early man might have looked and behaved are closely based on current research; children reading this book will certainly come away knowing a great deal about prehistory. But, more importantly, Dickinson asks questions – and provides some answers – about what he considers to be the true nature of all human beings. Children themselves have always had a soft spot for prehistoric times, and not just because of dinosaurs and other outsized distractions. It was also a world where the divisions between adults and children were much less clear than is true today, when every child must go through at least eleven years of formal education before having any serious claim to be treated as an adult. The children in this story are given far more responsibility much younger – something that will not be missed by today's young readers, always on the lookout in their fiction for stories that show how well the young can function, particularly in times of crisis.

**9 to 11**

## The Machine Gunners
**Robert Westall** (author)
Macmillan (pb)

Chas McGill is quite enjoying his experience of World War II up in the industrial northeast of England. There is shrapnel to collect most days, and always the chance that his school will be closed owing to bomb damage. Then one day he and his gang stumble across a crashed German plane complete with an intact machine gun. Prising it off, they install it in their specially-constructed hideout and use it to threaten Rudi, one of the plane's pilots, when he limps into their den. They soon get on well, however, and they are happy to harbour him until his ankle heals and he can make a run for it. They bring him food, but eventually things become too much, and when some vicious fighting breaks out Rudi is accidentally shot.

In this fine story, warfare itself is gradually stripped of any glamour or excitement and revealed for what it is – a tragic and brutal business, best avoided at any age. Robert Westall himself grew up in Newcastle during

World War II, and his memory for what happened at
the time, including the violence that affected everyone,
is razor-sharp. He shows that children might well have
enjoyed some of the new freedom available to them in
wartime, but he also shows how his characters
eventually come up against problems far too big for
them to deal with on their own. As in William
Golding's haunting fable, *Lord of the Flies*, what starts as
a game ends as a murderous shambles. The author does
not blame the children for the disaster that finally
happens. Rather, he seems to be blaming neglectful or
unloving parents and, above all, war itself – a time
when violence is legitimized as a way of life, so
tempting children into brutality themselves. War is no
longer glorified in children's fiction as was once
sometimes the case – particularly during the war years
themselves. Even so, it would be hard to find a story
more anti-war than this one, even though it also
concedes that there were still some moments of
pleasure as well.

## A Parcel of Patterns
**Jill Paton Walsh** (author)
Puffin (pb)

Life is really quite good in the little seventeenth-century
village of Eyam in Derbyshire, with Mall happy to dream

9 to 11

about the handsome young shepherd Thomas who is courting her. But the arrival from London of patterns for some new dresses also brings tragedy, for within that same parcel are the germs of the dreaded plague. Soon the village is so badly hit that its citizens decide they should not leave it, for fear of spreading the infection further. Those that try to break this rule soon find out that other surrounding villagers are sending them back at gunpoint. Mall refuses to see Thomas any more because he lives outside the village and she hopes to save him from infection. He is so insistent, though, that she is forced to send him a message saying she is dead. This leads to further tragedy, but in the end the village just about survives and some bitter hatreds are finally buried along with so many of the villagers themselves.

The author uses old-fashioned words and phrases throughout, making an already engrossing story – itself based on what actually happened in the real village of Eyam – seem even more convincing. But the issues she raises are eternal ones, relevant to any period of history: about whether lying can ever be justified; the relative importance of the individual versus the group; what qualities differentiate those who stay firm from those who crack; and whether in times of crisis what divides people is ultimately less important than what brings them together. There is much to think about in this story and much to feel also, especially when Mall's wretched plight finally becomes clear.

## Smith

**Leon Garfield** (author) **Antony Maitland** (illustrator)

Puffin (pb)

Twelve-year-old Smith, already a successful pickpocket in the streets of eighteenth-century London, happens

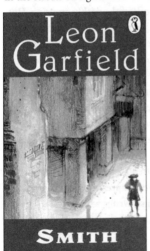

by chance to see a murder taking place. This proves to be very dangerous knowledge, and although he manages to shake off the killers who are now intent on silencing him, he is never free from them for long. Arrested and locked up in Newgate Jail on false charges, he breaks out on the night before his execution, using an old ventilation system to make his escape. When he reaches the top his enemies are waiting there for him once again, but Smith has survived for so long on his wits that nothing is going to stop him. In his possession he has a document which he knows is important even though he is unable to read it himself. A blind

9 to 11

magistrate, his only friend, also becomes involved. The climax, involving highwaymen, a coach and a cold, snowy graveyard just outside London, is as exciting as anyone could wish.

Leon Garfield was a masterful writer, who brought dead streets and long-past events to life in a way that remains vivid and also constantly, darkly amusing. He also felt strongly about the existence of poverty and its numbing effect on those caught up in it. In all his stories, he stands firmly on the side of the individual who – however unprepossessing on the outside – can still have a warm heart and a generous nature within. Garfield's villains, on the other hand, often come over as initially attractive people with their fine clothes or good looks. But readers eventually learn not to be taken in by such superficiality, given that it is what people do that really matters. Children themselves, still often inclined to judge from first impressions, can learn a lot from this novelist, who also writes wonderfully – coining new metaphors and playing with old ones in a constantly inventive way. Some have found his language a little over-the-top, but for others it stands as a source of continual delight. Children should have the chance to make up their own minds on this issue, either by reading this book or else turning to some of the many other enthralling stories this author has written about eighteenth-century Britain, like *Black Jack*, *Devil in the Fog* or *Jack Holborn*.

## A Traveller in Time
**Alison Uttley** (author) **Faith Jaques** (illustrator)
Puffin (pb)

Although Penelope lives in the middle of the twentieth century, she periodically finds herself swept back four hundred years to a time of political intrigue. This only happens when she visits Thackers, an ancient farmhouse owned by her uncle and aunt but once inhabited by the Babington family, loyal supporters of Mary, Queen of Scots against Queen Elizabeth I. Penelope knows that the plan to help Mary escape from the nearby castle where she is imprisoned is doomed to fail, but she is unable to make anyone else at the time believe her. Hidden tunnels and secret trapdoors known locally are still no match for royal spies, and her knowledge of the terrible events that are going to happen to people she has become fond of once they are captured causes Penelope to suffer in both centuries. Her story ends after a shattering climax where she very nearly loses her own life twice.

Written in 1939, this is a historical story in two senses, since its loving depictions of life in a very idealized mid-twentieth-century farmhouse seem almost as remote today as the descriptions of the same place four hundred years earlier. Having been brought up herself in the Derbyshire countryside, very near to where the Babington plot took place, Alison Uttley knew the area

9 to 11

intimately. And through convincing descriptions and telling detail she brilliantly conveys the essential continuity of country living over the centuries. The political and human drama going on at the same time is equally compelling, with Penelope leading a dreamlike existence in the past, sometimes able to communicate with others there, at other times condemned to be a silent witness. The author's fine autobiography, *The Country Child*, makes a perfect complement to this story: both offer modern children descriptions of the past made all the more vivid because they are written with such obvious affection.

## Witch Child

**Celia Rees** (author)
Bloomsbury (hb & pb)

When Mary's grandmother is hanged as a witch, unfriendly eyes turn on her granddaughter, since she also possesses some of the same healing arts. This is the seventeenth century, when witchcraft was suspected everywhere and many innocent people were put to death as a result. Running away just in time, Mary travels to America to start a new life in a Puritan settlement. But unfortunately the rumours travel with her, and the diary accounts she keeps describe how her enemies start closing in once again. Some of these are driven by spite rather than by any conviction that Mary actually is a witch; others notice that she does seem to have special powers that no one, least of all Mary herself, can really explain. The only support she has comes from a local Indian boy, despised by the self-righteous Puritan settlers who have already stolen his land away from him and his people. In a desperately tense conclusion, Mary escapes once again.

9 to 11

For very small children, witches still make some of the most frightening of all story-book villains. But history itself records that it was those who accused others of witchcraft who were in fact most to be feared, rather than the victims involved who were often little more than scapegoats for anything that went wrong in their communities. The author takes up this theme, showing child readers how easy it is to pick on those who live just outside society, even when they are doing a good job such as healing the sick. To one natural outsider, Mary herself, the author adds the figure of another, this time the boy, cruelly robbed of his birthright by Puritans using their religion as a cloak for colonial aggression. Since all children go through moods when they feel something of an outsider themselves, it is natural that they should sympathize with outsiders in fiction when these are presented in an understanding way. As well as offering an interesting glimpse of past history, *Witch Child* is an absorbing story in its own right. It is also very well written, using some of the language of the period in a way that is continually pleasing to the ear.

# School Stories

Children have always liked school stories, so long as such tales are lively and eventful. School is, after all, the place which pupils usually know far more about than do the adults in their lives. School stories, in their turn, reflect both the high moments of classroom comedy familiar to all pupils and also those darker times when individual children may fall out with particular teachers or else with the rest of their own age-group. This can result in bullying, and it is worth remembering that certain school stories – including some recommended here – were warning about the worst of these practices long before educational authorities began to take serious notice. Other stories concentrate on the strong loyalties that spring up between children, and the way that certain pupils can always seem to manipulate things to their own advantage whatever the opposition from

teachers, parents or other pupils themselves. Most school stories have little to say about actual lessons, choosing instead to focus on the whole restless, often unpredictable social scene that takes up the rest of the time.

### Blubber

**Judy Blume** (author)

Macmillan (pb)

**9 to 11**

Linda is certainly a very overweight pupil, but she only begins to be teased about this after the day she reads out an essay in class describing blubber, the thick layer of fat that lies under a whale's skin. This word is seized on as a nickname for Linda herself, with Jill Brenner, the narrator for this story, laughing as loudly as anyone. But when taunting turns to bullying, Jill decides at last to make a stand

against Wendy, the chief offender. But on arriving at

school next day Jill discovers that although the pressure is now off Linda it is on her instead. Suddenly she is given a new, unwelcome nickname, and is tripped up, has her satchel emptied and is ambushed in the school toilets. She only just manages to get out of this situation, and anyone who has ever been bullied at school will recognize the truth of this story.

There are also plenty of lighthearted moments in this excellent and compelling story about an important and often overlooked problem. There has never been a school without any bullying at all, but children who until now have taken a relaxed attitude towards the teasing of others may well think again after finishing this book. Young readers who have been seriously bullied themselves can also take some comfort from a story that seeks to bring such behaviour out from the shadows. There are no instant or easy solutions suggested here, though today more schools are developing anti-bullying strategies, and if any young reader attends a school that does not have one of their own, they could well ask their parents or teachers why not. But this story is about more than bullying; it also discusses the importance of staying detached at moments when group pressure to do something wrong may be at its highest. This is a lesson that can apply to many different situations in life, and Judy Blume does an excellent job in raising it quite so forcefully here. She is a hugely popular writer with young readers, and two

9 to 11

other of her books, *It's Not the End of the World* and *Superfudge*, both of which focus on some of the experiences of children growing into adolescence, are particularly recommended.

## The Chocolate War

**Robert Cormier** (author)

Puffin (pb)

9 to 11

Still one of the most explosive books ever written for young readers, this novel describes a kind of bullying which, far from being defeated (as normally happens in children's school stories), actually gets worse by the final page. Jerry Renault, a new boy at a Roman Catholic Secondary school in America, finds that he and everyone else is expected to sell up to fifty boxes of chocolates as part of a fundraising scheme devised by Brother Leon, the school's acting headteacher. But for this scheme to work well, Brother Leon realizes that he has to enlist the aid of the school's chief bully, Archie Costello, leader of a dreaded secret society known as the Vigils. In disgust, Jerry decides to opt out of the whole business, but then has to face the wrath of the Vigils, who stand to make money out of the sale themselves. With his mother dead and his father no real help, Jerry is very much on his own. After repeated goading, Jerry is set on by Janza, the meanest boy in the school. The book ends bleakly: Jerry is badly beaten and nothing much has changed.

Many young readers have since written to the author, thanking him for describing school as they know it themselves. As a skinny, undersized child, Robert Cormier knew bullying at first hand, both on his way to school and within the classroom from various unsympathetic teachers. He never forgot the experience, and his decision to end this story on such a bleak note reflects his determination to show readers what can happen when not enough good people decide to make a stand against wrongdoing by others. Such honesty was not always appreciated by critics at the time, and numbers of Cormier's books, including later titles such as *I Am the Cheese* and *After the First Death*, have even been banned in some states of America. It would be disturbing if all stories about adolescent life at school were as depressing as *The Chocolate War*, but it is right that at least one writer has made the decision to describe one pupil's time at school as his worst.

## The Demon Headmaster

**Gillian Cross** (author) **Gary Rees** (illustrator)

Puffin (pb)

There is something very wrong about the new school that Dinah is joining after being fostered by a local

9 to 11

family. All the pupils seem incredibly well-behaved, working during breaks and as good as gold in class. The headmaster is strange too; after looking into his sea-green eyes for too long, pupils find themselves doing whatever he wants – even when they are all massed together during morning assembly. Dinah too finds herself mindlessly repeating the slogans the headmaster has taught her without necessarily believing what they say. But then she discovers SPLAT – the Society for the Protection of our Lives Against Them – which is run by a few other pupils uneasy about what is happening at the school. They find out that the headmaster's next plan is to use some visiting TV cameras to hypnotize not just his own pupils but the entire country as well.

GILLIAN CROSS

THE DEMON HEADMASTER

What happens next is exciting, funny and raises some interesting questions about freedom. Why does the headmaster want such power? Readers are never told, indeed this mysterious figure doesn't even seem to have a name. And if this headmaster is quite so terrible, why is it that these stories about him have proved so very popular with children, both in book form and in the series subsequently written for TV? Is it the idea of pupils plotting against an unbending regime that is so attractive here, at a time when in real life all pupils are expected to work harder at school than ever before? These are questions readers may like to answer for themselves. They can also turn to more books in this series, or try some of the other titles by this brilliant writer – for example *Wolf and The Great Elephant Chase*.

### More of the Demon Headmaster

The Demon Headmaster
Takes Over
Revenge of the Demon
Headmaster

The Demon Headmaster
Strikes Again
Facing the Demon
Headmaster

## The Eighteenth Emergency
**Betsy Byars** (author)
Red Fox (pb)

Although Benjie is very bright he's still not clever enough to resist the temptation of making fun of classmate Marv Hammerman by writing his name under a picture of prehistoric man hanging up in school. Marv also happens to be the biggest, toughest boy around, while Benjie is so small he is known to everyone as "mouse". Marv lets it be known he wants a fight, so Benjie and his best friend Ezzie plot what to do next. In the past they have worked out how to respond to plenty of purely imaginary emergency situations, but this one – the eighteenth on Benjie's list – doesn't provide him with any easy solutions. He keeps trying to avoid Marv, but finally they meet in the playground after school where Benjie receives three large punches. No longer angry with Marv, he realizes that his original joke had actually been extremely wounding to someone who knows and constantly worries about the fact that he's not as clever as everyone else.

There are so many good moments in this story it is easy to forget its clear message of tolerance – Benjie has to realize that, puny as he is, he too has the ability to torment others through his ready wit and ability to make cruel jokes. But this is a story rather than a sermon. The author has an excellent ear for the cut and thrust of children's conversation, and although Benjie's dilemma is urgent enough there are some hilarious moments as well. American schools are in many ways different from those in Britain, yet there are similarities as well. Most readers will have come across a Marv by now, and perhaps after finishing this story they too may have a slightly better idea about what it might be like to

feel inadequate inside – however tough on the exterior.
If they are smart like Benjie, they may also come to
realize that it is sometimes better to hold your tongue
than make one crack too many at the expense of others.


## The Third-Class Genie

**Robert Leeson** (author) **Jason Ford** (illustrator)

HarperCollins (hb & pb)

Alec is having a bad day at school: he's late; in trouble
with his teachers; and threatened by one of the main
bullies. But everything changes when he discovers a
sealed beer can from which he hears the sound of
human snoring. Pulling the ring, he releases Abu Selem,
one of the Baghdad slaves of the lamp from the days of
Aladdin. Abu proves a considerable help in the days to
come – but something of an embarrassment as well. He
does Alec's homework on the Crusades
for him, but entirely from the
point of view of the
invaded Arabs. Alec's
history teacher takes
exception to this,
although readers
themselves may
well come to the
conclusion that in this

9 to 11

case Abu is in the right. One of Alec's chief tormentors is Ginger Wallace, leader of a black gang at the school. But when Abu is reported as an illegal immigrant, it is to Ginger that Alec turns for help.

The author has written many other books for children, and this is one of his best. Teachers, parents, pupils, friends and others all come across as real people with everyday concerns living in the sort of community familiar to city children. Life is sometimes tough, but relationships between the generations are often warm and supportive. Having a personal genie is one of those fantasies that children have always enjoyed in their fiction. But within this age group they can also understand and enjoy the humour arising from some of the potential awkwardness of this situation. E. Nesbit rang the changes on this particular joke in her excellent story *The Phoenix and the Carpet*, and in this book Robert Leeson proves himself a worthy successor. Both writers take a radical view in their fiction, questioning received opinion on a number of issues while maintaining a lively sympathy with child characters who want to do their best but somehow always seem to run into unforeseen disasters on the way.

9 to 11

## The Trouble with Donovan Croft

**Bernard Ashley** (author) **Fermin Rocker** (illustrator)

Puffin (pb)

9 to 11

Keith is getting on well at school, popular with his own gang of friends and always first to be picked for football in the playground. But everything changes when his kindly parents decide to take in Donovan Croft, a foster child whose mother has returned to Jamaica and whose father has to put in long hours at work. Donovan is so unhappy he retreats into total silence, and he is also black in a school where most other pupils are white. Some of these pick on Donovan – as does Keith's form teacher, who views the boy's silence as deliberate cheek. Keith is left in the position of having to defend his foster brother while feeling irritated and increasingly lonely himself. His own gang now turn against him, with taunts and fighting replacing former friendships. Donovan finally runs away; when he is found, he is gradually nursed back to normal life by his own father, his new foster parents and by Keith himself. In return, Donovan unexpectedly finds himself in a situation where he manages to save Keith's life.

Bernard Ashley was a London primary school headmaster and therefore knows a lot about modern children from first-hand experience. In this story he shows how deep unhappiness can sometimes make a child unreachable, in Donovan's case by turning him into what is called an "elective mute". Such a person can put an unbearable strain on all they come into contact with, since a total refusal to communicate can be extremely frustrating as well as very irritating. But one of the strengths of this story is its refusal to suggest that there are easy solutions to such serious personal problems. That is why Donovan ends this story improved but still not totally recovered. This is a realistic rather than a romantic ending, since personality damage, like physical injury, often takes some time and the right treatment before it can be brought under control – something young readers can learn while enjoying this taut and well-plotted story.

## The Turbulent Term of Tyke Tiler
**Gene Kemp** (author) **Carolyn Dinan** (illustrator)
Puffin (pb)

Tyke is very fond of jokes at school, even though these

9 to 11

often end up causing trouble all round. Best friend
Danny Price, who is backward in lessons and can hardly
make himself understood, has a less developed sense of
humour. The two show a fierce loyalty to each other,
which exhibits itself when Danny is accused of theft. He
has in fact stolen a £10 note, but he is caught before
Tyke has a chance to put it back. Danny runs away from
all the pressure, but Tyke knows where he will be and
sees that he returns safely. A bigger crisis looms when
the school decides that Danny must go to a special
school. Tyke steals some examination papers in order to
provide some last-minute coaching, but although this
scheme is also discovered, enough has been done to
persuade the teachers that Danny should stay with his

friends. The story ends with Tyke falling off the school roof after yet another episode of mischief. But just beforehand, the big secret about Tyke that has been kept from the reader all this time suddenly reveals itself.

The hidden detail is that Tyke is, in fact, a girl – though few readers will have guessed this. It's a twist that provides proof of the way that so many of us continue to think in terms of gender stereotypes – if a pupil with an ambiguous name is shown behaving rebelliously at school we usually make the automatic assumption that they must be a boy. Watching the look of astonishment on a child's face when they get to the last page of this story is an experience not to be missed; seeing them frantically going back in search of any clues they may have missed is another. The author also writes sympathetically about those pupils who are always going to find lessons difficult. Danny has the extra disadvantage of poor speech, which gets worse when he is under pressure, and the decision to keep him on in normal education is not necessarily the right one. Readers may want to have their own say on this and on some of the other issues brought up by this bright, lively book, which is full of good jokes. They could look out too for the author's excellent *Gowie Corby Plays Chicken*.

## The War of Jenkins' Ear

**Michael Morpurgo** (author)

Mammoth (pb)

It is the start of a new term at boarding school, and thirteen-year-old Toby Jenkins is trying not to cry on the train journey that will take him there. He hates school and dislikes most of the other pupils, but a new boy called Simon Christopher appears who looks as if he might be a bit different. Toby gradually discovers that Simon does in fact possess extraordinary powers. He seems to be able to foresee the future while also making things happen simply by wishing them so. But what follows is not simply a lighthearted story about magic; Simon is also convinced that he is Jesus Christ reborn. He demands that Toby follow him in everything, and for some time Toby does just that. In the background there is an ongoing war between the "toffs", Toby's fellow pupils, and the "oiks", the scornful and jealous local village boys who live nearby. One of their sisters works in the school kitchen, and she and Toby fall for each other. A major conflict between the two gangs looms, which Toby just manages to head off at the last moment. Simon is involved too as a peacemaker, but shortly afterwards he is expelled from the school for having the cheek to suggest he is Christ come again to earth.

Is Simon really who he thinks he is, or is he just a

9 to 11

11 to 16

seriously muddled teenager? This remains an open question, because halfway through the story he does actually seem to possess supernatural powers of healing. But if Simon is a badly disturbed child and little more, it remains true that his influence on others is wholly good and the decision to expel him seems cruel from a headmaster who already has little to recommend him. Pupils like Simon with their own agendas to follow can be very difficult for any institution to accept, particularly when they disobey rules and insist on doing things their own way. But the fact that Simon is nearly always right might suggest that it is the school that should learn something from him. This is a story that simply demands to be read, not least because it provides a great deal to think about. Children could also look out for the same author's *Kensuke's Kingdom* and *The Butterfly Lion*.

# Fantasy Stories

Fantasy stories have recently gone through a boom period, with some excellent writers now entertaining not just children but often adults as well. Those tales chosen here range in mood from the light-hearted to the serious, with fantasy often used to explore future worlds where current freedoms are abolished and the environment threatens to become unsustainable. Because fantasy writing invents its own worlds and characters, it can issue particularly powerful warnings about certain world trends by depicting how such developments could conceivably end in a way that is disastrous for everyone. Other writers focus on themes like the possibility of time travel, or the implications of being able to work magic in an otherwise recognizably normal world. There are also comic fantasies, but even these often ask interesting questions along the way. Humans have

**9 to 11**

always used the imagination to test themselves out not just in reality situations but also in conditions that have so far never existed. Fantasy writing does the same thing, with the best of it providing moments of imaginary liberation young readers may well remember for the rest of their lives. While it is true that children need realistic stories in their reading diet in order to get some idea of what the world they are living in is actually like, they also have an abiding hunger for fantastical writing, where the normally solid and sensible surroundings they know so well are transformed into something unpredictable.

## Artemis Fowl
**Eoin Colfer** (author)
Viking (pb)

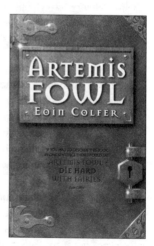

Artemis Fowl is a twelve-year-old boy with a prodigious intelligence. Unfortunately he puts this to use in various dishonest ways, leading up to his most daring exploit yet. This is no less than a plan to steal one tonne of fairy gold, something that has never been achieved before. To do this he needs to kidnap a fairy to use as a hostage, and this is what happens to Captain Holly Short of the Lower Elements Police Reconnaissance Unit. This resourceful leprechaun ends up drugged and imprisoned in a cellar after sadly underestimating her human opponent. But although superior fairy technology wins out in the end, the unpleasant Artemis still manages to come away with half his prize, and doubtless the promise of a return visit in the near future. Captain Holly, meanwhile, is reunited with the tough and world-weary fairy forces that have worked so hard to free her. The only real casualty is a marauding troll, treated as an enemy by both sides and finally dispatched despite his enormous fighting strength.

Billed as "Die Hard with fairies", this is not a story for the squeamish. A scenario involving kidnapping, semtex, drugged victims and orders to kill delivered by a remote army council is uncomfortably reminiscent of recent events in Northern Ireland. But there is no reason why fairy stories should always remain stuck in the past, and while some older readers may blanch at the idea of the little people armed with machine guns, young readers should have no problems here. This is because Colfer writes with humour while always developing his plot at a great pace. Ancient lore involving fairy forts, crossing thresholds and getting back before dawn are all integrated here into a modern world, while the book's set-piece scenes and imagery often draw their

**9 to 11**

inspiration from film and television rather than from a rural world of long ago. Although Artemis himself is an unpleasant character, both Holly and her immediate boss put saving lives before profit, remaining loyal to each other however politically inexpedient. The author's style, a mixture of informality and technical know-how, is constantly engaging.

## The Book of the Crow
**Catherine Fisher** (author)
Red Fox (hb & pb)

In this superb sequence of novels, the country has long been controlled by the sinister Watchmen who now run it like a police state. The only opposition to them comes from the Makers, who once used to be in charge and still dream of restoring their own civilized rule. They are represented here by Galen, the crabby but noble Master of the Relics, and Raffi, his young apprentice. There is also Carys, originally a spy from the Watchmen, and the Sekoi, a cunning, seven-fingered half-human, half-animal with an uncontrollable lust for gold. Together they travel through their stricken homelands, avoiding the Watchmen as best they can while still trying to spread the message of freedom.

There are four volumes in *The Book of the Crow* sequence, each one tense and exciting. Catherine Fisher

9 to 11

has an extraordinary imagination, always coming up with some new twist that is both weird yet utterly convincing. Though the world she describes is not ours, it does have strong similarities to some of the war-torn and tyrannical countries that sadly still exist today, offering a memorable and frightening glimpse of what life must be when there is no freedom of thought. The books' vision of a polluted landscape is equally powerful, carrying a strong warning for all countries that neglect their long-term future for the immediate concerns of the present. Such themes are only part of this quartet of stories, since each one also focuses on different aspects of the tension that exists between an old, fading leader and his young, sometimes restless, apprentice. They also touch on the perennial problem of how characters can trust each other in a hostile environment when doing so may often be extremely risky. The author has written many fine fantasy stories for children, all stimulating and challenging as well as immensely readable. *The Book of the Crow* is her finest achievement so far.

### The Complete Book of the Crow

| | |
|---|---|
| The Relic Master | Flain's Coronet |
| The Interrex | The Margrave |

## Charlotte Sometimes
**Penelope Farmer** (author) **Chris Connor** (illustrator)
Red Fox (pb)

Falling asleep on her first day at boarding school,
Charlotte wakes up to find that the girl in the bed next
to her is not the
person who was there
the evening before.
Looking out of the
window, she sees that
the view has
changed too. Slowly
she realizes that she
has somehow
slipped back in
time to the same
school forty
years before.
The other girls
now address
her as Clare,
but after spending a
somewhat troubled day
with them Charlotte
wakes up next morning with everything back to
normal. During her day away she has been replaced at
her modern school by the real Clare from the past, who

**9 to 11**

looks almost exactly like her. This pattern keeps repeating itself during the rest of this haunting story, with Charlotte leading two quite different lives but managing to correspond with Clare across time through a hidden diary they both resolve to keep. Eventually Charlotte makes a discovery about Clare which changes everything, but not before she has spent large chunks of time in the past. Returning to the present means she has to abandon Clare's younger sister Emily, but there is one more major surprise still to come.

This dream-like story is both moving and thoughtful, combining as it does two popular conventions of children's literature – the ideal companion and travelling back in time. Whether they are interested in history or not, children usually have a strong awareness of the past because photographs and family stories tell them that their own parents and grandparents were once as young as they are now. One satisfaction of all "time slip" stories such as this is that they enable a child to imagine witnessing events that occurred long before they existed. This story starts by feeding this fantasy before gently insisting that ultimately everyone must stay in the times within which they were born and be satisfied with that.

## Earthfasts
**William Mayne** (author)
Hodder (pb)

9 to 11

Two boys, Keith and David, are out on the Yorkshire
moors together towards the end of an evening when
they start to feel the ground stirring beneath them and
hear the distant sound of drumming. A moment later
both boys start trembling, for out of a nearby hill
marches Nellie Jack John, a drummer boy from the
eighteenth century who still thinks he is living back in
those days. Called "Nellie" because he is the son of Jack
who was in turn the son of Nellie, the drummer boy
angrily denies he is a ghost. Instead, it gradually turns
out that he is the victim of a strange mix-up in time.
The hill he comes out of also contains King Arthur and
his sleeping knights, who now begin to stir as well.
Other strange things also start to happen: ancient, dead
giants appear, and ordinary pigs turn into dangerous
wild swine.

By the end of the story, Nellie is reconciled to living in
modern times, working at a local farm where he's
become popular with everyone. And although he comes
from a different century, the author shows how in this
very traditional part of Britain language and farming
methods have altered so little that Nellie has few
problems settling in. Told largely in dialogue, this is
also one of those stories where readers have to fill in the

various gaps in the narrative for themselves. Some may find this story too much like hard work. But it is so skillfully told that all the information readers want is always there – like an extended conversation, it is simply a question of waiting until all the bits fall into place. The reward, when this happens, is a sense of especial closeness to the action of the story. The two sequels, *Cradlefasts* and *Candlefasts*, continue the story to its dramatic conclusion. The author, who lives in Yorkshire, is fascinated by local dialect and legends. He has written many other books for children, but this series remains his most popular.

## The Dark is Rising
**Susan Cooper** (author)
Penguin (pb)

"When the dark is rising, six shall turn it back; Three from the circle, three from the track." And so it turns out, when Simon, Jane and Barney Drew suddenly find themselves pitched into a terrible battle between good and evil. But their great-uncle Merriman knows all about this struggle, and that it has actually been going on for thousands of years. Whenever the forces of darkness seem about to win, a great leader like King Arthur will appear to keep the balance once again. A schoolboy on his holidays finds that it is he who has the

9 to 11

power to resolve this grim battle after accidentally discovering an ancient manuscript of huge importance to both sides. With the aid of the rest of his family, he sees off the danger in *Over Sea, Under Stone*, the first book of this riveting sequence. But there are still four more titles to come each one racking up the

tension until the old prophecy is at last realized: "Wood, bronze, iron; water, fire, stone; Five will return, and one go alone."

The author is expert at creating suspense where it is least expected; after finishing these books, even a reader's next journey outside might momentarily seem loaded with meaning and possible danger. While the starting point of these stories are the kind of fantasies a child might have, Susan Cooper elaborates them with the sort of detail and plot refinement that would be impossible for most children ever to make up for themselves. That is why, at nearly 800 pages, *The Dark is Rising* is still not long enough for her many fans.

## The Dark is Rising Sequence

Over Sea, Under Stone
The Dark is Rising
Greenwitch

The Grey King
Silver on the Tree

## His Dark Materials
**Philip Pullman** (author)
Scholastic (hb)

When Lyra's friend Roger suddenly disappears, along with other a number of other children, she knows she has to find him. Setting out with her daemon – a visible spirit that takes the form of an animal and which everyone in Lyra's world possesses – she enlists the help of some local river gypsies who have also lost children. Their travels take them to the bleak lands of the North, where she discovers some strange and sinister scientific experiments taking place, in which her own mother, the attractive and powerful Mrs Coulter, seems closely involved. As for her father, Lord Asriel297, is he out to save the world or is he someone who has developed too much of a taste for power?

These and other questions are explored throughout

the three magnificent novels that make up this series. The action takes place in a number of different, parallel worlds – including our own – which resemble each other but also have many profoundly different characteristics. In the second book Lyra meets up with a boy called Will in what becomes a quest to save the world from a dictatorship where no one is allowed to think or act independently. Pullman draws his inspiration from archetypal myths, as well

**Philip Pullman**

**His Dark Materials**

The award-winning trilogy:
*Northern Lights*, *The Subtle Knife* and
*The Amber Spyglass* in one volume

as from Milton and Blake, to create an extraordinarily rich but often violent universe. At the same time, a cast of weird but completely convincing characters helps push a complex and gripping plot to a point of almost unbearable suspense. The author is a wise as well as highly gifted writer, and he provides readers with much to think about as Lyra and Will stumble from one crisis to another, never totally sure what they should do but always unafraid to put themselves in danger. This is a book in which quantum physics and gnosticism rub shoulders with armoured bears who talk and knives that can cut their way from one world to another. But all these rich and diverse elements are brilliantly woven together and, although written fairly recently, there seems little doubt that *His Dark Materials* is already established as a classic.

## His Dark Materials Trilogy

The Northern Lights          The Amber Spyglass
The Subtle Knife

**9 to 11**

## The Lord of the Rings
**J.R.R. Tolkien** (author)
HarperCollins (hb & pb)

This huge volume, numbering over a thousand pages, has captivated readers of all ages ever since it first appeared in 1954. Its hero Frodo is a hobbit who, like his Uncle Bilbo Baggins before him, is small in body but great in courage. It falls to him to find and return the magical and all-powerful ring to its true home deep in the mountains, but if the hobbits' many enemies find it first, that will mean the end of them and their civilization. Frodo therefore decides to start out on a long journey in search of the ring accompanied by a chosen group of friends, with his actual route carefully mapped out by the author at the start of each section. Tolkein's control of detail is such that he invents entire languages for the people Frodo comes across, and a host of wonderfully unforgettable characters throughout. The world in which all this happens is often something like ours, both in the beauty of its countryside and in the terror of its occasional devastation. But within its boundaries, whole lands are laid waste by a tyranny with the power to turn everything into dust and ashes.

*The Lord of the Rings* became something of a cult after it was published, but it is not necessary to take the various dwarves, elves, dragons, wizards, orcs and goblins that throng these pages too seriously in order to enjoy the author's masterly control of plot. Yet Tolkien believed utterly in the importance of what he was doing. Although his fiction has no direct reference to Christianity, the author (himself a devout Christian) felt that the ability to believe in an imaginary universe was part of the same impulse that enabled humans to sustain religious belief. And he saw his stories – and fairy stories in general – as preparing readers for belief in the "other world" of Christianity. It is this quality of total belief that gives these stories their mesmerizing power – along with many moments of high adventure, often mixed with a quiet humour.

# The Other Side of Silence
**Margaret Mahy** (author)
Puffin (pb)

Hero, the name of the young heroine in this story,
certainly has problems. Everyone else in her family talks
so much that she has decided to give up all speech
herself in protest. Her mother, a nice but rather bossy
expert on child behaviour, doesn't know what to do
with her. Hero herself passes much of the time
climbing from tree to tree in her big garden. One day
she lands in the territory of the family's middle-aged
neighbour, Mrs Credence, also somewhat strange and
given to wearing her dead father's black cloak and hat.
Once there, Hero finds it difficult to break away,
particularly because she knows there is a dark secret in
the top room of Mrs Credence's sinister house.
Sneaking up there on her own, she makes a terrible
discovery, and is discovered herself by Mrs Credence.
Luckily, everything has been witnessed by her brother
Athol – who turns out to be her saviour as well.

Based loosely on an old fairy tale, this is a story of
tremendous power. In her writing for older children,
Margaret Mahy specializes in novels where the fantasy
element often becomes more real than reality itself. In
doing so, she responding directly to those young
readers who also spend much of their time imagining
things about themselves and others. In this novel, for

9 to 11

example, an old lady imagined to be a witch actually turns out to be one. The girl who discovers this secret is saved at the last moment by the modern equivalent of a prince riding to her rescue. Her powers of speech restored, she is now ready to start a new life after what looks very much like a spell upon her finally loses its force. The author has written many other unforgettable novels for this age group, in particular *Underrunners*, *The Haunting* and *The Changeover*.

**9 to 11**

## The Owl Service

**Alan Garner** (author)

HarperCollins (pb)

An English family are spending a holiday in Wales, in bed and breakfast accommodation run by Gwyn and his mother. To begin with the visiting teenage boy and girl get on well with Gwyn who is their age, but gradually the tension rises. All these characters, adults and children, eventually come to seem doomed to repeat an ancient story associated with this particular valley, where jealousy and hatred have once before led to a final murder. A clue to understanding this myth is found in a strange dinner service hidden away in the loft of the holiday cottage. When the plates are arranged one way, they form the figure of a menacing owl. But if they're moved, the picture turns into a mass of flowers. As the atmosphere darkens further, Gwyn finds out a terrible truth about his own origins and it looks as if a tragedy is unavoidable. But myths from the past do not necessarily have to repeat themselves in the present; just as the dinner service itself can change, so too can an almost impossible situation – given sufficient strength and understanding.

Alan Garner is an electrifying writer; this is one of those stories that can be read over and over again, with further layers of detail becoming clearer each time. He believes that myth is crystallized experience handed down over the ages, and that authors today should draw on this ancient wisdom while also bringing it up-to-date by incorporating it into modern stories and symbols. Such stories may not always be easy to read at first, but Garner also thinks that what we feel most deeply cannot always be spoken in words. Powerful images, however, can always connect with readers, and all his stories contain messages that transcend the actual events shown to be taking place. Any story by this extraordinary writer is worth reading, whether it is one of the earlier adventures like *The Weirdstone of*

**9 to 11**

*Brisingamen* or later works like his magnificent *Stone Book Quartet.*

## Paulina
**Lesley Howarth** (author)
Walker Books (hb & pb)

**9 to 11**

Rebecca and her family are on holiday in America, having exchanged their cottage in Britain for a luxurious house complete with Buick and swimming pool. But who is this waif called Paulina who delivers newspapers to them that are sixteen years out of date, and whose cheap pink plastic belt keeps appearing in various places in the house and garden? And why does an exercise bike in the basement start working by itself along with other ghostly sounds and sightings? The local teenagers are also a problem, congregating round the pool for an uninvited party at night and leaving debris everywhere after they leave. It is in fact the pool that provides the clue to all this mystery: it turns out that Paulina had once been a swimming champion and does not want any visitors enjoying what she still sees as her own special space. But what is even stranger is that she fell to her death sixteen years ago – at around the same time as all those old newspapers.

Children usually enjoy ghost stories, and this one should be no exception. But the ghost here is a bit different, since in every other way she is no more than a very ordinary teenager with an attitude problem. She's also the type of ghost who comes back to complain about the bad treatment she experienced when alive. Members of the British family in this story have not themselves misused Paulina, but she has had an unhappy life and it is only when Rebecca understands this and gives back to her what she was looking for that everything finally calms down. Lesley Howarth is one of the best children's writers around, with a striking ability to entertain as well as provoke thought. Other books by her include the no less stimulating *Mister Spaceman* and *Maphead*.

## Playing Beatie Bow
**Ruth Park** (author)
Barn Owl (pb)

Abigail Kirk lives in Sydney, Australia. One day, after giving chase to a mysterious younger girl with a strangely old-fashioned look, she finds herself transported back to the same place a hundred years ago. Adopted into a family originally from Orkney and who seem to be expecting her, Abigail now has to learn how to live the life of a poor immigrant in the nineteenth century. She dislikes the heavy clothes she is expected to wear, and once almost gets kidnapped by a gang after wandering off down a notorious back alley. While Abigail always wants to return to her own time she gradually comes to like and respect the family she is living with. But things get complicated when she realizes that she has fallen for Judah, the handsome, nineteen-year-old son. There is also the matter of the psychic gift that Abigail appears to have, whereby she seems to have been singled out to do something of vital importance for the family before she can finally return to her own times.

Time travel books often present a relatively rosy view of the past. This one is very different, with Abigail appalled to begin with by the primitive sanitation and poverty which surround her. Out on the streets she sees manacled convicts shuffling past, while at home upstairs there is a child suffering from an illness no one has any idea how to cure. This vivid sense of a past that is frequently alarming to modern sensibilities is exceptionally well-caught in this story, as are some of the compensations that are shown to exist as well. The family she stays with is consistently kind and caring, and while life has its share of horrors, these simply don't compare with the advanced technology of warfare and slaughter that exists in Abigail's own lifetime. When Abigail finally returns home she is a calmer, more reflective person. A final ingenious twist in the story reminds readers that whatever we think might happen in the future, nothing is ever going to be certain. First published in 1980, this book remains unforgettable and deeply impressive for readers of all ages.

## Shadow of the Minotaur

**Alan Gibbons** (author)

Dolphin (pb)

Phoenix hates his new school where he is forever being teased about the name his Greek-loving father chose for him years ago. So it is tempting for him to escape from this unpleasing reality as often as possible into The Legendeer, an amazing video game his father has been asked to try out at home. Its special effects seem the

**9 to 11**

best yet – until Phoenix realizes that they are so good they are actually real. Getting into the game gradually becomes easier than getting out, with a hideous Minotaur not just a figure on the screen but also a genuine presence out to kill Phoenix and anyone else in his way. When best friend Laura also disappears into the

game and cannot extricate herself, it is time for Phoenix to come to the rescue in the shape of Theseus, the ancient hero of legend now having to fight his battles all over again.

It is no surprise that Greek myths continue to play an important part in contemporary literature; they make up some of the most unforgettable stories ever, not just in their surface detail but in the way they respond to basic human desires that have hardly changed over the centuries. In this story the Minotaur could be said to stand for the ferocious and animal side of human nature that all civilizations have to curb if they are going to remain reasonably stable. But driving such violence underground does not mean that it necessarily disappears for good. The story of Theseus and the Minotaur can be seen as a fable about the constant battle between the forces of light and darkness that takes place within every individual as well as within society as a whole. Others have explained this particular legend differently, but one of the defining qualities of myth is the way it can always signify different things to different people. And whatever its ultimate meaning, a myth can still pack enormous power, as it does in this suspenseful story, which ingeniously combines details of the ancient world into a convincing modern setting.

## The Sterkarm Handshake
**Susan Price** (author)
Scholastic (hb & pb)

Halfway into the twenty-first century, the rulers of the world have at last developed the necessary skills to be able to visit the past on a regular basis. Passing through a type of time tunnel, special messengers can now go back and forth to the fifteenth century in a couple of minutes in order to do some useful trading with what is still an unpolluted and comparatively unexplored landscape. But those they trade with, a tough border clan known as the Sterkarms, gradually come to resent the patronizing way in which they are treated. Andrea, a

young researcher on a visit herself to the past, sympathizes with them; she also falls in love with Per, the brave young son of the clan leader. Things get difficult when Andrea decides she is too much of a modern woman to put up with the sexist and brutal behaviour she comes across while living in the past. She decides to return to her own time, only to be pursued by Per, who cannot bear to let her go. He finds himself thoroughly out of place in a modern urban environment which to him seems without beauty or soul. And by now war has broken out between the armies of the two different times.

This is a brilliant story – thoughtful, eventful and moving all at once. It shows the dangers existing in an overdeveloped, modern society, revealed here as having lost touch with all morality when it comes to dealing with others. So while going back to the past is not really a solution – even though in this story it's possible to do just that – staying in the present may be equally difficult for those who do not fit in and show no likelihood of ever being able to do so. This would seem rather a despairing message, but it is made palatable here by the continual excitement of a plot where something is always about to happen, to characters who are so real that they feel like friends. The nature of the story also allows the author to comment upon those undesirable colonialist attitudes heard within our own times, but this parallel is merely suggested rather than underlined in a story that never lets up for a moment.

## Tom's Midnight Garden

**Philippa Pearce** (author) **Susan Einzig** (illustrator)
Puffin (pb)

Tom really doesn't want to stay with his uncle and aunt during the summer holidays, but there is no choice. They live in a flat in a converted, shabby old house with no access to any garden. But all this changes when Tom wakes up one night after the big grandfather clock downstairs unexpectedly strikes thirteen times. Looking out of the window, he sees there is now a beautiful garden outside. Later on he watches three older boys playing in it, followed by a smaller girl, Hatty, also dressed in old-fashioned clothing. Tom would like to join in, but this

9 to 11

is impossible because he seems to be invisible to them – a sort of ghost, in fact. But Hatty does eventually see Tom, and promptly sticks out her tongue at him. Later they make friends, but each time they meet Hatty has grown older. Finally, on a skating trip up the frozen river that flows at the end of her garden, she and Tom start to fade to final invisibility in each other's eyes.

First published in 1958, *Tom's Midnight Garden* is one of the finest children's books of all time, dealing directly with the strange and fascinating notion for children that the very old must once have been young too. As for ghosts, these are no more than ordinary people who can somehow be seen by others living at a different period of time. Once Hatty and Tom get to know each other, they become firm friends since both are lonely in their own lives. But however appealing this idea is, the author shows that time can never really be defeated. Tom eventually accepts that he can no longer stay indefinitely in the magical garden, and that his ghostly presence there is no longer needed by Hatty once she has a life of her own. The questions he asks himself and others meanwhile about time itself and what it all really means arise naturally from the narrative and stay in the mind long after this haunting story is finished. Philippa Pearce followed this charming and sympathetic book with several other triumphs, including *A Dog So Small* and *The Battle of Bubble and Squeak*.

## Witch Week

**Diana Wynne Jones** (author) **Tim Stevens** (illustrator)

HarperCollins (hb & pb)

"SOMEONE IN THIS CLASS IS A WITCH". This note, which appears between two of the Geography books Mr Crossley is marking, has to be taken seriously because although the date is 1981, this is a society where witches are still dangerous – and still burned. Larwood House is a boarding school that accepts a number of witch-orphans, but if pupils show any sign of taking after their parents they could be in real trouble with the Inquisitors, not to mention the local police. But instead of this problem quietly disappearing, it soon looks as if there might be two witches in the class, or even more. When an arrest is made it is time for worried pupils to get help and,

9 to 11

summoned by a spell learned from an elderly witch in retirement, Chrestomanci – the elegant wizard who understands everything – now appears on the scene.

One reason why *Witch Week* is so good is because its author avoids the overblown language typical of some fantasy writing; instead her children talk and act like the real thing – sometimes good-humoured, sometimes cross, but all the while occupying a quirky magical world full of surprises. She is also aware that too much easy magic – like too much of anything – can quickly pall, so she keeps things interesting by introducing certain restrictions: her witches and wizards are able to work their magic in some situations, but remain helpless in others. By creating magic with such a recognizably human face, Diana Wynne Jones ensures that readers will enjoy the best of both worlds, the real and the imaginary. One of the most brilliant writers of her generation, all her books deserve to be read. Nothing else remotely like them exists in children's literature. Within them she creates a world that is constantly intriguing as well as highly dramatic, written with sparkling intelligence throughout.

## The Chrestomanci Series

# Animal Stories

Favourite books about animals for this age group tend now to be subtler than before, with fewer obvious jokes and a greater sense of seriousness. The animal characters within them are usually less obviously anthropomorphic, often caught up in genuinely fraught situations they can barely control. Sometimes principal animal characters behave exactly as animals would; at others they show human sensitivities while still preserving the typical behaviour patterns of their species. Human characters often feature, frequently as an animal's main support but sometimes as the enemy. In some cases animals are depicted as living within their own communities and having as little to do with humans as possible. All the stories recommended below tackle the problem of how to create convincing animal characters – usually in a way that is compassionate and sympathetic.

Animal stereotyping is common: those animals depicted as essentially noble or faithful tend to be horses, dogs or lions, while animal villains are usually drawn from vermin, although in the case of Robert O'Brien's fine novel it is the rat characters who emerge as the true heroes.

## Black Beauty
**Anna Sewell** (author)
Everyman (hb) Penguin (pb)

11 to 6

Black Beauty is born a handsome foal; but it's what happens to him after he leaves the pleasant meadows of his youth that the book is about. All goes well to begin with, but as he grows older some careless handling ends up reducing his value as a riding or carriage horse. Instead he is relegated to dragging a cab round London in the days before the arrival of the motor car. There he meets his old friend Ginger, also a cab horse but now no longer with the will to live. The scene of Ginger's eventual death is one of the most powerful and moving in all children's literature. Things are not much better for Black Beauty himself – nor are they for his human owner, the cab driver Jerry Barker, who must also stay out in all weathers in order to earn the money he and his family so urgently need. But just when things look most desperate, the horse is recognized by his former groom, and is taken back to live out his old age in the countryside.

The author of this book was disabled and therefore very dependent on horses for travelling. She felt strongly about the cruelty and neglect of animals that she often witnessed, and wrote this book in 1877 to try and change attitudes. It had an enormous influence at the time, and eventually led to a law banning the "bearing reins" that were used to keep horses' heads fashionably high but which also caused them great pain. By a cruel irony the horses drawing the hearse at Anna Sewell's funeral were still wearing the reins she hated so much, and reform did not take place until a few years later. The strength of the book is that it is never simplistic: although there are some unpleasant characters in the story, cruelty to animals is most often presented as part of an evil system rather than as the fault of a few individuals. No straightforward answers are given to the problems the author writes about, and this is another novel that shows older children how few moral issues are quite as simple as they seem. But the author's own contribution also demonstrates that wrongs can be righted and bad laws changed – and that such changes can greatly improve the conditions of those unable to speak up for themselves.

9 to 11

## The Mouse and his Child

**Russell Hoban** (author) **Lilian Hoban** (illustrator)

Faber (pb)

This extraordinary story is about a tin clockwork mouse and his child, joined by the hands and designed to dance under a Christmas tree. They do this for five years until one day the family cat knocks them over and breaks them.

Thrown into a dustbin, they are rescued and repaired by a tramp, who then walks off, leaving them to find a safe place of their own. Their quest occupies the rest of the story and involves great danger, chiefly from their main enemy Manny the Rat, who smells "of darkness, of stale and mouldy things, and garbage". He is the local thief, gangster and bully, who talks in menacingly soft tones. Somehow the mice must outwit him in their search for the friends they once knew in the toyshop, where there was also a magnificent doll's house they now want to make their home.

9 to 11

This wonderful story is as fine as any of the fairy tales written by Hans Andersen. The father and son's determination to find a permanent place to live will ring bells with child readers still heavily dependent on the security of a stable home themselves. And philosophical teases scattered around the text, such as the search for the ultimate dog (based on a picture of a dog that contains in miniature the same picture – apparently ad infinitum), present just the sort of intellectual challenge that young readers now often enjoy. But above everything else, it is the strange, funny-sad atmosphere of this story that children will probably remember most, where every passing animal or insect character has a point of view but no one ever quite seems to know what really matters.

**9 to 11**

## Mrs Frisby and the Rats of NIMH
**Robert C. O'Brien** (author) **Justin Todd** (illustrator)
Puffin (pb)

Mrs Frisby is the head of a family of field mice. When her son Timothy falls seriously ill it becomes important to move him somewhere safe, but where? Her own little house is going to be demolished as soon as the local farmer starts ploughing. But after going to an old owl for advice, she is told to contact some remarkable local rats who might be prepared to help. To her great surprise she discovers them living in neatly furnished accommodation complete with its own supply of electricity, which comes in very useful when the rats want to read books or papers. They are clearly a super-breed, the result of being caught by human scientists in order to be put through various experiments in a laboratory simply known

by the initials "NIMH". The regular injections they received there increased their intelligence so much that eventually they were able to read and act upon the directions posted up on how to open their own cages. When they finally escaped, they resolved to build a new civilization, harvesting their food instead of stealing it as before. But there are still human enemies to consider, and Mrs Frisby herself ends up saving them from a planned gas attack.

Rats almost always get a bad press in children's stories, but they are pictured in this one as both intelligent and family-loving. It is the human characters who come off badly – especially those who think they have the right to experiment on animals. This is of course a very hotly-debated issue, with the opponents of animal testing increasingly vociferous and sometimes violent. Children will have to make up their own minds about this argument, and a book as intelligent and sympathetic as this one offers an excellent way to introduce them to the issues. It also places children in the unfamiliar position of seeing the world from the point of view of a species that is usually reviled. This sort of surprise can in itself be stimulating, particularly at an age when children are beginning to think along more speculative lines than before. The author's daughter, Jane Leslie Conly, has written two good sequels: *Rasco and the Rats of NIMH* and *RT, Margaret and the Rats of NIMH*.

## National Velvet
**Enid Bagnold** (author)
Mammoth (pb)

When Velvet Brown wins a piebald pony in a village

raffle, no one is very impressed – least of all her butcher father. He thinks the pony should be slaughtered for dog's meat, but Velvet knows better. Although it doesn't move very quickly, she soon discovers that it is a marvellous jumper. And slowly the idea forms: why not enter him for the Grand National? She consults her best friend Mi Taylor, a young man who works in her father's business and who is himself obsessed by horses. Together they concoct a letter to the race organizers, and as this particular race is open to all comers, the pony – now registered as

Enid Bagnold
*National Velvet*
a Classic Mammoth

National Velvet – is duly included as a runner. Velvet wants to ride him herself, but women jockeys are not allowed. So Mi cuts her hair short – and wearing ordinary riding clothes in order to pass for an apprentice male jockey, the moment eventually arrives and she mounts her horse at the starting point.

This was the first of what later turned into a flood of pony books aimed at young readers, and it remains easily the best. It also contains a great deal of detail about life in the prewar countryside. But it is probably the theme of horse riding that has particularly appealed to readers ever since the book was published in 1935. Its story offered girls in particular an image of themselves as tough and effective – a welcome change from the stereotyped female passivity prevalent at the time. And the sheer physicality of the horses depicted in this story also provides plenty of excitement. On another level the idea of winning against all the odds can thrill readers who like to imagine themselves doing the same sort of thing in their own lives. A Hollywood film later followed, but the book has an energy all of its own and still deserves to be read.

**9 to 11**

## Tarka the Otter

**Henry Williamson** (author) **C.F. Tunnicliffe** (illustrator)
Puffin (pb)

"The eldest and biggest of the litter was a dog-cub. His fur was as soft and grey as the buds of the willow before they open at Eastertide. He was called Tarka." Enter one of the best-known of story animals – brave Tarka, king of the river until he is hunted down and killed by a band of otter-hunters. Before that, we follow Tarka through his daily routine of fishing, eating and sleeping, getting to learn all his favourite spots and coming to recognize his other friends and rivals. There is also the first meeting with his mate Greymuzzle, with whom he eventually has a family.

The author knew every stretch of the river he describes in this book, which is set in North Devon. At one time he also reared a baby otter himself after the mother was shot by a farmer. This type of intimate knowledge helped create one of the best stories about nature ever written. Children's authors describing wildlife often humanize animal characters by giving them speech and sometimes clothes as well. Others, however, try to describe what real life might be like in the wild for animals whose own thought processes are of course extremely difficult, if not impossible, to describe convincingly. Williamson opts for the latter strategy, which means that this is a novel virtually without any dialogue at all. Tarka behaves like the wild animal he is, killing ruthlessly when there is the need – even when this means the death of a beautiful swan. Readers with a

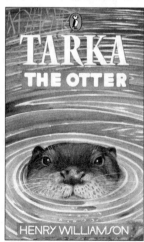

sentimental view of animal existence can learn a lot here, not just about otters but also about river life in general. They will also acquire some knowledge about the cruel practice of otter hunting, now banned but once a regular occurrence in the Devon countryside.

## Toad Rage
**Morris Gleitzman** (author)
Puffin (pb)

No one seems to like the Australian cane toad. Not a naturally good-looking animal, it also spits out white pus at anyone who threatens it. But Limpy (so called because of his squashed leg), a particularly thoughtful toad, is determined to improve the image of himself and his fellow animals – in the hope of stopping all the lorry drivers who deliberately try to flatten them on the roads. Limpy decides he will become one of the three mascots chosen by the Australian athletes' team competing at an international games event in South Australia. Since all these mascots will be selected from Australian wildlife, why not choose a cane toad as well? Along with his friend Goliath (who's huge in size if not in brains), the two friends hike down South running into many different adventures on the way but always just managing to survive. Thoughts of their favourite food – worm stew with slug topping – keep them going when there is little to eat and their spirits are low. Finally they, and all other overlooked animals, decide to organize their own Non-Human Games.

The author is one of the funniest currently writing for children, but as with many other amusing writers he has a serious purpose as well. Limpy, despised because of his looks and habits, is in fact very intelligent with an attractive personality. It is wrong that he should be judged on his appearance alone, and this point will not be wasted on young readers used to judging others on first impressions without bothering to go any deeper. An ecological point is made here as well. One reason that cane toads are looked down on is that they are not indigenous to Australia's wildlife. But in a country with a huge immigrant population, is there any good reason not to show tolerance towards immigrant animals as well?

9 to 11

## Watership Down
**Richard Adams** (author) **David Parkins** (illustrator)
Puffin (pb)

The main character in this compelling story is Fiver, a rabbit with a highly developed sense of danger. Sensing that something dreadful is about to happen to the warren where he lives, he manages to persuade his brother Hazel and a few other friends to leave before it's too late. They are only just in time: human beings, their greatest enemy, are about to come in and destroy their living space to make room for their own developments. Roaming the Berkshire countryside in search of a new home, the rabbits encounter many dangers – not least railway lines, roads and rivers as well as normal predators. But they keep their spirits up by telling stories drawn from their own stock of myth and legend. At last they find a good place to settle, but first there is

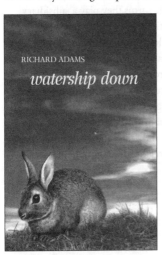

RICHARD ADAMS
*watership down*

a bitter fight with another colony of rabbits who are ruthlessly organized and savagely aggressive. By now the main characters of the wandering rabbit band will have become deeply familiar to readers – Bigwig, Blackberry, Dandelion, Silver, Groundsel, Bluebell and many others.

The author, who was also a keen natural historian, knew a lot about rabbits, and much of what happens in these pages has close parallels with what is going on in the countryside

**9 to 11**

today. The story began as a tale told to his own children, drawing on local scenery well-known to the family. It is also partly based on those traditional epic stories where a group of close male companions is forced to wander from place before finally reaching a permanent place of safety. Numerous battles and adventures take place in such tales, so giving each of the males involved a chance to prove their courage and loyalty. There are female animal characters in this story too, but as in most epic forms they play a subsidiary role, leaving all the action to the males and otherwise keeping an extremely low profile. Some readers have resented this sexual imbalance, but for others this is still a good story with a strong feeling for nature. There is also the constant interest in seeing the human world entirely through animal eyes, with the result that even objects like cars and trains come over as monstrous. Reading this story can only raise the awareness of children about man's relationship with the natural world.

# Stories from Home and Abroad

Fiction set in our own times can be particularly challenging for writers, since if they get anything seriously wrong young readers will quickly spot any errors. The advantages are that children will come across stories that closely reflect their own situations and experiences, or those of their friends. The stories selected here range from descriptions of common domestic upheavals to accounts of unique events in an individual's life. Other stories are set abroad, reminding readers that while local scenery, conditions and ways of living can be very different, human beings themselves are often similar to each other. While the chief characters in these stories are usually children, there is also much about those adults who play an important part in their lives. Sometimes such adults are shown as unpleasant and even dangerous, but by this age young readers will already know that such people exist, and that some children have very difficult lives. Stories that emphasize the problems of society may often help to shed light on what can otherwise seem quite inexplicable to children, while usually carrying a final message of hope at the same time.

## The Diddakoi
**Rumer Godden** (author) **Creina Glegg** (illustrator)
Macmillan (pb)

"Diddakoi" is the name given to a person who is half gypsy, which is what Kizzy Lovell happens to be. And because she lives in a caravan and wears clothes that smell of wood smoke she is teased by the local children, many of whom have been brought up to despise anybody who lives outside conventional society and who travels from place to place. Kizzy in her turn thinks that these village children have their own peculiarities – why else would they allow dogs into their houses or use the same washing bowl for clothes and

dishes? But after Kizzy's last remaining relative dies she is eventually given a home by Miss Brooke, a middle-aged newcomer to the village. To start with things are difficult, with Kizzy refusing to eat and deliberately flooding the bathroom. But Miss Brooke sticks it out, and for a while all goes well until some really vicious bullying at school leaves Kizzy almost dead. More adventures follow, with peace finally restored when Kizzy is allowed her own personal caravan in the back of Miss Brooke's garden.

While there used to be plenty of romantic descriptions of gypsy life in children's literature, this is one of the few novels that show how tough it can be to live as an outcast. Rumer Godden knew a lot about the life of modern gypsies, and wrote her book to help

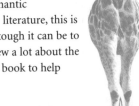

others understand them better. In a broader sense, the story is also about the need for tolerance for all those who follow a lifestyle is seen as unusual. Such people often face prejudice simply because they happen to be different. Few books can actually change such attitudes without help from other quarters too, and some children may well finish this book with their negative views confirmed. But it is important to raise such issues with children which can then be discussed afterwards, either at home or in the classroom, and few stories do so as clearly and directly as this one.

## Gold Dust
### Geraldine McCaughrean (author)
Oxford (pb)

Inez and her brother Maro are very surprised to see a big hole dug outside their father's shop in the Brazilian town where they live. To make matters worse, other holes start appearing too, until the main street itself more or less disappears. The reason for all this activity is gold, or at least the hope of it, which initiates a modern-day gold rush as greedy and frantic as anything that took place in California all those years ago. But eventually the madness ends, leaving Inez and her brother with the feeling that at times adults can behave a good deal worse than children.

Geraldine McCaughrean is one of the most original of modern children's authors, with each new book completely different from anything she – or anyone else – has written before. This story describes what happens to poor people once the prospect of untold wealth opens out before them. Rumours, raised hopes and lies all fan the flames of greed; others, meanwhile, set about using the situation to their own advantage, whether any gold is eventually discovered or not. The author does not condemn the people who are prepared to dig up their whole town in a frenzy to be first where the gold· is. Rather, she shows how certain individuals can keep their heads in such situations – in this case Inez and Maro. They end the story determined to go for the longer-term gains of education in preference to any dubious schemes about getting rich overnight. The author has written other fine stories, in particular *Forever X*, about a sinister hotel where it is Christmas every day of the year, and *A Little Lower Than the Angels*, which describes how a young stonemason, fleeing from his cruel master, takes up with some travelling actors.

## Handles

**Jan Mark** (author)
**David Parkins** (illustrator)
Puffin (pb)

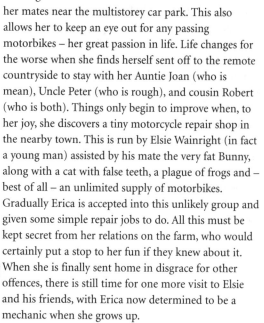

9 to 11

Erica Timperley is a girl who loves messing around with her mates near the multistorey car park. This also allows her to keep an eye out for any passing motorbikes – her great passion in life. Life changes for the worse when she finds herself sent off to the remote countryside to stay with her Auntie Joan (who is mean), Uncle Peter (who is rough), and cousin Robert (who is both). Things only begin to improve when, to her joy, she discovers a tiny motorcycle repair shop in the nearby town. This is run by Elsie Wainright (in fact a young man) assisted by his mate the very fat Bunny, along with a cat with false teeth, a plague of frogs and – best of all – an unlimited supply of motorbikes. Gradually Erica is accepted into this unlikely group and given some simple repair jobs to do. All this must be kept secret from her relations on the farm, who would certainly put a stop to her fun if they knew about it. When she is finally sent home in disgrace for other offences, there is still time for one more visit to Elsie and his friends, with Erica now determined to be a mechanic when she grows up.

Children's stories set in the deep countryside usually concentrate on describing the beauty of the surroundings and cataloguing the instinctive wisdom of those who have always worked there. Jan Mark, herself always something of an unruly and rebellious author, will have none of this. Erica is very much a town girl who does not want to be in the country and never gets used to the idea. She is also very much her own person, rejecting more conventionally feminine pastimes in favour of motorbikes. While she remains unpopular with her country relatives, she does succeed in making friends with the offbeat characters in the shop, thus moving from the position of lonely outsider to an accepted insider. Readers of either sex will find themselves cheering her on at this stage, given that they too may already have had some experience of falling out with their own families over particular likes and dislikes. Jan Mark is not the easiest of writers but she is always completely believable – as well as very funny. Among her other quirky books are *Thunder and Lightnings*, *Nothing to Be Afraid of* and *Trouble Half Way*.

9 to 11

### Holes
**Louis Sachar** (author)
Bloomsbury (hb & pb)

Because his whole family has always suffered from bad luck, Stanley is not really surprised when he is found guilty of a theft he never committed and sent to Camp Green Lake, a boys' juvenile centre stuck in the middle of the Texan desert. In fact there is no lake there and not much green either – only sand, baking sun, rattlesnakes and scorpions, with the nearest water supply over a hundred miles away. To make matters worse, every boy there is required to dig a deep hole each day in ground so hard it is barely possible to break into it with a spade. Stanley gets down to it, since the alternative is cruel punishment handed out by the pitiless chief warden, a terrifying woman whose nails are coated in rattlesnake venom. The reason she wants the holes dug is that for years she has been searching for some valuable jewellery that she knows is hidden somewhere in the area. Working his way through blisters and aching muscles, Stanley eventually makes some good

9 to 11

friends and decides to escape.

This book occupies that uncertain territory between fantasy and reality, giving it the quality of a dream that sometimes turns into a nightmare. But while conditions are appalling in the Camp, the inmates themselves are shown treating each other better than they are treated by the staff. Young readers are spared the full horror of what can happen in real-life juvenile institutions where bullies often rule the roost and quieter children like Stanley sometimes have a very bad time indeed. But although this story has a happy ending, it is a reminder of what can happen to young people who fall out with the law and are sent to places remote enough for the rest of society to have very little idea what goes on in them. Other quite different themes also crop up in this extraordinary book – like the way the past can influence the present and the importance of keeping faith with friends. This is such a powerful story that readers are unlikely ever to forget it.

## Homecoming

**Cynthia Voigt** (author) **Sharon Scotland** (illustrator)

HarperCollins (pb)

Thirteen-year-old Dicey is left in a car park with her three younger siblings when her mentally disturbed mother finally wanders off, never to return. So with

hardly any money – and not knowing what else to do – the children set off to find a hitherto unknown aunt who lives over a hundred miles away and whose exact address is unknown. Sleeping rough at nights and getting by with the minimum of food during the day, things begin to look really bad when their money finally runs out. Eventually a kindly student listens to their story and agrees to drive them the rest of the way. But even when they meet up with their aunt, there are still plenty of adventures to come before they reach

safety and security with another unknown relative.

Young readers often imagine what it would be like surviving on their own, but this novel shows just how very tough it can be when parents disappear and children have to fall back on their own resources. Any romantic ideas about running away are likely to be squashed by this story, which goes into detail about how difficult it is to find somewhere warm and safe to sleep, let alone money in order to eat. Fortunately the children never meet anyone who preys on the young, but the narrative is dominated by an awareness that things could go very wrong. This novel proved so popular on first publication that the author went on to write more stories about the family. But this is undoubtedly her masterpiece: one of those books children can learn from while enjoying a totally gripping narrative at the same time.

**9 to 11**

### The Tillerman Family Cycle

Homecoming
Dicey's Song
Seventeen Against the
    Dealer

Come a Stranger
A Solitary Blue
The Runner

## The Illustrated Mum

**Jacqueline Wilson** (author) **Nick Sharratt** (illustrator)
Doubleday (hb) Yearling (pb)

Marigold is an unusual single mother. She is covered in tattoos, often forgets to buy food and sometimes stays out all night, leaving her two daughters on their own. And occasionally she has been known to "borrow" someone else's credit card without asking first. For all that Marigold is still a loving mother and when she is

in a good mood everyone has a great time – often doing quite unexpectedly fun things such as painting the walls of a room in the colours of the sea or suddenly making biscuits in the middle of the night. But at the age of 33, Marigold is beginning to feel the strain of her poverty, dashed hopes and messy surroundings. Her oldest daughter Star finally leaves home to stay with her long-lost father, while Dolphin, the younger daughter, also sets out to find her different father, who has not seen her since she was a baby. What will happen to Marigold if and when she is finally left on her own?

It is a mark of an excellent writer that a character like Marigold can be made to seem sympathetic despite her many faults. But

Jacqueline Wilson is always honest as well as compassionate, and Marigold's essentially destructive nature is not glossed over – especially in those few moments when she comes over as dangerous as well as eternally self-deluding. Even so, it is also made clear why the younger daughter Dolphin remains so attached to her mother. Who else, after all, would ever be likely to show her half as much love and affection, however weirdly these feelings are sometimes expressed? But once the two lost fathers turn up, Marigold's days as the sole parent in charge are numbered, and the story ends with no clear indication of whether she will ever get her life together again.

Children reading this story will learn a lot about the nature of a child's attachment to a parent. They may also notice that if the same parent is also a bit odd, such attachment can at times be all the stronger on the part of a child desperate to protect the person they love most in the world. Jacqueline Wilson often describes the sort of characters so easily condemned for their behaviour by others who have made no effort to understand them. Particularly recommended in this category are *The Story of Tracy Beaker*, *Double Act*, *The Suitcase Kid* and *The Bed and Breakfast Star*. But although she sometimes writes about depressing subjects, her stories are never dispiriting themselves, always containing excellent jokes no matter whatever else is happening.

9 to 11

## Journey to the River Sea

**Eva Ibbotson** (author)

Macmillan (hb)

**9 to 11**

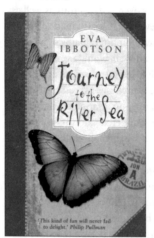

Maia, a thirteen-year-old orphan, is told that she has to leave her school in Britain in order to join some distant relatives who live hundreds of miles up the Amazon River in Brazil. She looks forward to her new life there – until she discovers that the members of the family expecting her are only interested in the money she will bring in. Fortunately Miss Minton, the outwardly fierce governess who travels with her, manages to protect Maia against the worst excesses of a pair of objectionable twins and their equally unpleasant parents. But life soon gets better when Maia starts making friends with the local Indians who eventually lead her to Finn, a child her age with a mysterious past and an uncertain future. After many more adventures – including a magical boat trip to the very heartland of Brazil – Maia, Finn, her governess and a boy actor she meets all find the happiness they deserve. Her villainous British hosts, on the other hand, are eventually exposed and then punished for their greed and dishonesty.

This story is set in the year 1910, but in truth neither time nor logic play a large part in this author's unique style of storytelling. Part fairy tale, with Maia very much a Cinderella figure, the main impression readers will be left with is one of an extended daydream, with the Brazilian jungle providing a suitably exotic background. But such obvious fantasy material does not entail any overt sentimentality, and some of the details that slip in every now and again are almost shocking in their unexpected bluntness. At heart, though, this is a story about a perfect young heroine who soon meets a small group of others as good as she is herself. Those who oppose her come over as coarse and nasty and without any redeeming features. Such melodrama always has a place in fiction, particularly when writing for children in those moods when they want everything to work out happily at the end of an exciting story. The author has extensively researched this remote part of the world, and her knowledge of it shines through these pages, particularly in those moments when Maia can afford to relax in order to drink in all the timeless beauty with which she is surrounded.

9 to 11

## Kit's Wilderness

**David Almond** (author)

Signature (pb)

**9 to 11**

Kit Watson has just moved to Stoneygate, an old mining area now facing hard times. Local children are unwelcoming at first, and his own grandfather is seriously ill. But a new friend soon comes Kit's way, warning him about a dangerous teenage initiation rite involving a pretend burial. Not joining in is considered cowardly, but it is a terrifying ordeal that Kit has to endure as best he can. Gradually he becomes aware that the whole area is haunted by the memory of a dreadful mining accident in the past. His grandfather knows something about it, and so too does a mysterious presence that seems to light Kit's way when he becomes trapped underground. His chief enemy during this time is a local boy from a difficult family. When the boy goes missing, Kit realizes that he has to find him in order to heal ancient wounds that have festered too long.

David Almond is fascinated by the way that the past constantly impinges on the present. He describes an area of north-east England with a once thriving industrial past that has now virtually vanished. People remain in the grip of the past, however, clinging on to long-held enmities between families while only having the haziest understanding why such bad blood existed in the first place. Now with his grandfather dying, Kit realizes that it's up to him to discover some of these past secrets and try to put an end to the hatred that goes with them.

Moving into a tight, new community always involves a trade-off between remaining separate and making reasonable accommodation with others, but this balancing act is made harder when one requirement is to do something so dangerous as to be life-threatening in itself. There is plenty more to stimulate young readers before this fine story is finished. David Almond's ability to make events seem as if they were actually happening is also in evidence in *Skellig*, a bestselling children's novel that is also widely read by adults.

## Madame Doubtfire

**Anne Fine** (author)

Puffin (pb)

Lydia, Christopher and Natalie are used to their parents quarrelling, even though they are now divorced and living apart. Neither is ever entirely right or wrong: Mum does most of the work but is tough to live with, while Dad, who is affectionate and funny, never gets round to doing very much at all. But he is extremely fond of his children, so when his ex-wife advertises for a daily help while she is out at work the idea suddenly

hits him: why not dress up as a middle-aged lady and apply himself? It is just as well that his former wife is short-sighted, since he gets the job and is soon back to his old ways in his former house – the children, of course, having seen through his disguise from the first minute. For a while things are easier all round, until ex-actor Dad pushes his luck too far and is finally unmasked.

Parents in the course of splitting up do not usually provide much cause for comedy so far as their families are concerned, and there are moments in this story when each child is shown going through the awful experience of divided loyalties. Yet because the Dad here is also a natural clown, there are some very funny moments as well. But even as they are laughing, children – whether from broken families or not – will also be learning about the way that two ordinarily intelligent people once in conflict can both become quite convinced that it is they and not the other who has complete right on their side.

The truth is that while both parents here do have a case to argue, they are both so oblivious to the faults each possesses as to make it impossible for them ever to live together in harmony. So while this story rejects any idea of a final reconciliation, it does show that when family breakdowns happen there are better and worse ways of dealing with them. Coming across a funny, gripping, moving and brilliantly readable story such as this will help young readers understand some of the mysteries of adult relationships while richly entertaining them at the same time. There's a film version of *Madame Doubtfire*, but it's nothing like as good as this brilliant book. Anne Fine has written many other superb stories for children such as *Goggle-Eyes*, *Flour Babies* and *Step by Wicked Step*.

## Make Lemonade
**Virginia Euwer Wolff** (author)
Faber (pb)

Lavaughn, a bright fourteen-year-old, seeking some after-school jobs in order to save up for university, answers an advertisement for a babysitter. As a result she meets Jolly, a single mother of seventeen, who already has one child as well as a new baby. The flat is a mess, and neither child is potty-trained, but Lavaughn decides to take everything on, despite the way Jolly

makes fun of her posh name. Gradually Lavaughn makes friends with the children and with their mother, who though disorganized is good-hearted enough. After being unjustly sacked from her job, Jolly decides to get some more education – which will also mean free childcare. But first she has to be persuaded to take this step by Lavaughn, and many quarrels ensue before Jolly eventually attends class and, after a slow start, begins to do well. There are always money problems, though, and Lavaughn must try to get on with her own schoolwork too. But one day a lemon seed she originally planted for the older child actually turns into a young plant – a symbol of the new life Jolly is slowly making for herself and her children.

**ff**

## Make Lemonade
Virginia Euwer Wolff

'This book has to be read. Don't miss it!'
*In Brief*

This is a story of poverty and neglect but also of hope and love. Help comes to Jolly in the unexpected shape of a girl still at school, and the story of their relationship and its frequent ups and downs is entirely convincing. Jolly is lucky to find such a friend, but Lavaughn in her turn also benefits from being with the children. Seeing for herself at first hand the importance of getting the sort of education that will stand her in good stead in the years to come is another important step in her development. When her own mother finally gets involved with the family too, it seems that everyone comes off better as a result. Although it is aimed at adolescent readers, younger ones should certainly be able to enjoy and understand this book, which is written as if by Lavaughn herself and all the more convincing for that. A sequel, *True Believer*, continues the story but this time with more focus on Lavaughn and the various problems that beset her during a difficult adolescence.

## The Other Side of Truth

**Beverley Naidoo** (author)

Puffin (pb)

Two shots at the gate in the early morning, and a car screeches away down an avenue of palm trees. For Sade and her ten-year-old brother Femi, this is the beginning of a nightmare – their mother has been murdered and their father forced into hiding. They are the victims of a

cruel West African government, out to silence anyone who dares to criticize the injustices that occur every day. Sade and Femi are eventually smuggled to Britain for their own safety, but they are then abandoned by those who were paid to help them. With no money and

**9 to 11**

nowhere to stay, the two children are soon picked up by the British police. By now they have decided not to say anything about themselves, in case this gets their father back home into even more trouble. Taken in by a kindly foster-home, the two children start going to school where there is more trouble from a gang of bullies. But just when things seem at their worst, there is contact with their father and the family comes together once again.

This is a fine and challenging story about children who are also asylum seekers. Comment in the press is often harsh about such people, but this novel shows how important it is to help those who through no fault of their own are in terrible danger in their own countries. Reading this sensitive and believable story is likely to make young readers feel more positively towards asylum seekers; they may also find themselves wondering how they would manage were they to find themselves alone in a foreign country with no money or contacts. Born in South Africa, the author has written other excellent stories with an African setting, in particular *Journey to Jo' burg* and *No Turning Back*.

**9 to 11**

## Pig-heart Boy
**Malorie Blackman** (author)
Corgi (pb)

Young Cameron has a heart that is badly damaged by a viral infection. In order to survive he must have a transplant, even though this means using a pig's heart because no human replacement organ is available. Although this operation has not succeeded before, he and his family gradually get used to the idea – though not before plenty of arguments about it. Others outside the family are not so accepting, and Cameron finds himself at the centre of press and television interest when he would much rather be left on his own. Some of his own friends are also uneasy with the idea, making remarks that would have been better unsaid.

**9 to 11**

Finally the great day for the operation arrives – and it fails to work.

Written with understanding and plenty of wit – even when the going gets tough – *Pig-heart Boy* takes a young audience through some of the main arguments for and against such operations. Although trying to remain united, Cameron's parents cannot help their disagreements occasionally coming to the surface, while his grandmother is quietly dismissive of the whole idea. This leaves Cameron with the final decision to make for himself. Children are more frequently consulted these days before undergoing serious surgery, but the book suggests some of the difficulties this can entail. Cameron's reasoning, coupled with the conflicting advice he receives, is always made clear throughout, with readers almost coming to feel part of the decision-making process themselves. Malorie Blackman is a highly popular novelist for young readers and her stories *Hacker* and *Thief!* are no less dramatic and involving.

## The Secret Diary of Adrian Mole aged 13³/₄
### Sue Townsend (author)
Mandarin (pb)

Adrian Mole is a real worrier, and every single anxiety

is recorded in his diary. Spots on his face, his parents' rocky marriage, his passion for his usually unavailable girlfriend Pandora, school, friends, a very stupid pet dog – all these and many other subjects are discussed, analyzed and complained about page after page. Although he may deny that he is feeling jealous, inferior or angry at any particular moment, it is always obvious from his particular choice of words when Adrian is deceiving himself. There are many excellent jokes, usually at Adrian's expense, and some moments when everything goes exactly as he wishes. But however optimistic he occasionally feels, the reader knows that he will soon revert to his normal moaning.

Children younger than Adrian should enjoy this peep into the mysterious world of teenage life, in the belief that things can't be as bad for them as it seems always to be for him. He is one of those characters with an ability to make other people feel better about themselves, given that it's rare for anyone in real life to be such a consistent loser and also such an eternal optimist. Adrian might so easily be an entirely pitiable character, and there are indeed moments of pathos in his story. But his habit of believing so totally in his grandiose fantasies – added to his marked inability to learn from his many mistakes – ensures that he's one of the great comic characters of recent times. Readers of any age who laugh at him are also in a sense laughing at themselves too, since most of his failings are wholly

recognizable. In this way, Adrian is often a mirror as well as a clown, and as such he's fascinating – especially to younger readers.

### The Continuing Saga of Adrian Mole

The Growing Pains of
  Adrian Mole
Adrian Mole: the
  Wilderness Years

Adrian Mole: the
  Cappuccino Years
Adrian Mole: from Major
  to Minor

## The Snake-Stone
**Berlie Doherty** (author)
HarperCollins (pb)

Jamie always knew that he was adopted. But as he gets older he begins to wonder why his first mother had given him away, leaving him with only a tatty old envelope bearing an address that is almost impossible to read. There are also growing demands on Jamie to be a champion diver, and at times he is pushed too hard for his own good. When he begins quarrelling with everyone at home as a result, he decides he must find out what happened years before. All this time, Jamie's biological mother is also telling her own story in separate sections of this novel. The result is highly gripping, and though the story comes up with no ideal

**9 to 11**

solutions to everyone's problems, there is still a sort of happy ending as Jamie finally comes to terms with the complexities of his life.

Many young readers will be fascinated by the idea of seeking out a long-lost parent, however secure they may be within their homes. The notion that a mysterious father or mother is somewhere out there crops up regularly in myths and stories of all kinds. But for those

who have reason to be genuinely confused about their origins, romantic daydreams often come second to the need to know more about their biological parents as a means of better understanding themselves. To what extent are such children the product of their adoptive parents who took them in, and to what extent might they still share some of the same physical and psychological traits of their original parents? Novels like this help answer such questions while also gripping readers in

9 to 11

what is perhaps the greatest drama of all: the search for a character's basic origins. The author deals with this issue cogently and sympathetically, and readers should also look out for her *Dear Nobody* and *Granny was a Buffer Girl*, both equally compelling.

## A Thief in the Village and Other Stories

**James Berry** (author)

Puffin (pb)

James Berry was born in Jamaica, and these stories tell of the country life he got to know there. The thief in the title story is thought to be Big-Walk, a strange, silent man who has been given this name because he has a habit of leaving his hut for weeks and then just as suddenly returning again. When chickens and piglets start disappearing, he gets the blame – chiefly because he has never bothered, or been able, to make any friends. Guarding their coconut plantation one night when their parents are away, Nenna and her brother Man-Man hear a noise. Man-Man fires off his shotgun, and running forward both children find blood on the ground near a bag of stolen coconuts. Big-Walk is arrested as the obvious suspect, even though there is no evidence against him. But at the last moment the thief turns out to be Duke, a popular town-man who lodges with the schoolmaster. Big-Walk is released, silent and

9 to 11

friendless as ever, unable to change because that's the way he is.

Other stories, also told in a mixture of Jamaican dialect and everyday English, describe hurricanes, a pet mongoose, a child-led craze for mouth organs and a horse that escapes drowning by a near miracle. Although there is some occasional sadness, reading these stories is rather like walking straight out into the warm sun. But they are never sentimental: the characters involved have weaknesses as well as strengths, and their poverty is sometimes hard for them to bear. Visitors to modern Jamaica would find a country very much more up-to-date than the one described here. But although conditions change, people tend to stay the same, and this collection overflows with instantly recognizable types and characters.

## The Village by the Sea
**Anita Desai** (author)
Puffin (pb)

In the village of Thul, on the west coast of India, Hari and his sister Lila are the two oldest children of a family in which the mother is ill and the father (a former fisherman) is nearly always drunk. With no work available, Hari runs away to Bombay to earn some money, leaving Lila to cope with two younger sisters on

her own. While Hari finds work as a dish-washer, Lila has to deal with her father's creditors. There are no miracle solutions; the mother gets worse, finally moving to hospital, and the children must work very hard for what they get.

Anita Desai stayed in Thul for many of her holidays, and she writes vividly about the daily events there and the sort of people she got to know. Her story ends on a note of change, with a big fertilizer factory opening near the village offering more jobs but also spoiling much of its natural beauty. Whether this represents a good or bad thing for the likes of Hari, Lila and the other young people living in Thul now and in the future is left unclear. The author herself takes a neutral position, but because there are no easy answers, readers are left with plenty to think about in a story that also shows how much children can achieve – even when the odds seem so hopelessly stacked against them.

# Poetry

Many fine poets have written for children, and some of the most outstanding are included below. Reading through a selection taken from the same poet provides an excellent introduction to the art of poetry itself, once the particular characteristics of an individual style gradually become apparent. Also recommended are a number of modern anthologies, which contain no prevailing style of presentation or predictable choice of subject matter. Editors no longer believe that children at this age range should be as sheltered in their literary experience as was once the case, so although there are still poems about such child-friendly topics as pets and holidays, there are also ones that address some of the more complex issues and emotions that children may be beginning to understand for themselves. All the anthologies recommended below are designed for the bedside

rather than the classroom, to be dipped into only when the time is right and the mood is willing. Parents who remember how boring poetry anthologies at school once seemed should certainly sample these collections as well, joining their own children in what can now often prove a fascinating voyage into new realms of the imagination.

## Falling Up
**Shel Silverstein** (author/illustrator)
HarperCollins (hb)

The title of this collection comes from a typical Silverstein fantasy concerning a little girl who, after tripping over her shoelace, finds herself falling up rather than down. This poem sets the scene for the rest of the book, illustrated by the poet himself with the same degree of manic delight that infuses his poems. An American humourist with several other books of verse to his credit, he manages to remain both amusing and stimulating at the same time.

The games he plays with words should remind children of the time when they too used to react to metaphors as if they described the literal truth – so in the poem "Short Kid", for instance, the victim finds nothing surprising about the fact that a foot is growing out of the top of his head since everyone had said that "I'd grow another foot". Another young character who unwisely asks an old witch to "make me a sandwich" finds that this is exactly what happens, with an accompanying picture showing a worried-looking sandwich perched on two little legs. Other poems ask different, sometimes more serious, questions: "I said, 'I'll take the T-bone steak.'/ A soft voice mooed, 'Oh, wow.'/ And I looked up and realized / The waitress was a cow." This particular theme is repeated elsewhere "There once was a hamburger whose name was James – / What? Didn't you know all burgers have names?" A few poems are a bit sinister, but on the whole the prevailing mood is one of high-octane craziness, as in "Millie McDeevit screamed a scream / So loud it made her eyebrows steam." With so many brilliant British poets for children around, it would be easy to miss equally fine ones from abroad. Silverstein is exactly that: very clever, distinctly odd and endlessly interesting. He is also an excellent draughtsman, which means that the pictures here often take the poems to a stage well beyond the actual words on the page.

## I Like This Poem

**Kaye Webb** (editor)

Puffin (pb)

9 to 11

As chief editor of
Puffin books from
1961 to 1979,
Kaye Webb had
an unparalleled
understanding
of children's
reading tastes.
To this was
added her own
unquenchable
enthusiasm for
literature at its
best, so well
displayed in this
particular
anthology. It is
also unique in that the poets and many of the poems
within it were actually selected from over a thousand
recommendations made by children themselves. Entries
arrived from a variety of different schools all over
Britain as well as from abroad; the poems were then
arranged according to the average age of the children
who had chosen them, beginning with verses selected

by six- to seven-year-old children and progressing up to the choices made by readers aged fifteen.

It is always difficult to predict what type of children's literature will prove most attractive to a defined age range of young readers, and this is particularly so in the case of poetry. This anthology begins with an extract from Shakespeare that readers of any age could enjoy and ends with William Blake's "Reeds of Innocence". But what is particularly novel here is the inclusion of extracts under each poem from the letters sent by children explaining the reasons for their choices. The little girl who chose the witch's chorus from Macbeth, writes that she did so "because in the part 'fire burn, and cauldron bubble' it makes me think of volcanoes erupting…'snake, bake' sounds like the fat in the frying-pan spitting. 'Frog, dog' sounds like Mummy's cake ingredients going thud in the bowl.'"

On the whole, the younger children involved in this anthology seem charmed by what they describe as the "funny words" and "good rhythms" in poems, particularly those about animals. Children around nine and ten become more interested not just in the various jokes that poems play but also in poems that describe different people and places. Eleven-year-old children, by contrast, seem more into the world of feelings, hidden meanings and unusual, beautiful phrases. The result of their combined choices is a wonderfully eclectic collection ranging from Pam Ayres to Andrew

9 to 11

Young. Atmospherically illustrated by Antony Maitland, this book has stayed in print since it first appeared in 1979 and deserves to remain so for many more years to come.

## The Rattle Bag
**Seamus Heaney & Ted Hughes** (editors)
Faber (pb)

Assembled by two of the leading poets of our time, this collection is for everyone – whatever their age. Poems appear in alphabetical order according to their titles or first lines, with the name of the poet only appearing at the end. There is no attempt to group poems by theme, so that the exact nature of each contribution is never predictable, but some wonderfully odd conjunctions of poems appear – like D.H. Lawrence's "The Piano" followed by Hopkins' "Pied Beauty" – which suggests a certain artful humour in the selection. Poems range from familiar masterpieces to rare discoveries, including some translations and numbers of traditional, anonymous poems drawn from oral culture.

A glossary of unfamiliar words appears at the back, but otherwise this book simply presents poetry for what it is, spurning any accompanying illustrations and with no editorial comment apart fromm a half-page introduction. Seen as a long-term investment, this anthology richly deserves its place on any bookshelf. Even those poems only half-understood by children can still sometimes hold a certain fascination, if only for the sounds of their words and the beat of each line, and many will return to this collection again and again.

## The Ring of Words
**Roger McGough** (editor)
**Satoshi Kitamura** (illustrator)
Faber (pb)

This anthology draws mostly on twentieth-century poets, and has a particular atmosphere of unpredictability and excitement. It's divided into ten loosely-themed sections, so that "Kicking Up the Winter" contains weather poems – several of them about winter – while "Thoughts Like an Ocean" concentrates on poems about the sea. Illustrated with quirky drawings by Satoshi Kitamura and using large print throughout, it is an extremely child-friendly anthology, seldom including more than one poem on each page and with the emphasis upon humour and adventure rather than anything more solemn. One of the disadvantages of having a major poet as editor of an anthology can be that he or she will be too modest to include any of their own work. Not so with Roger McGough who chooses himself more than anyone else, but since he is such a brilliant poet – especially for children – who could quarrel with his decision?

## Selected Poems for Children
**Charles Causley** (author) **John Lawrence** (illustrator)
MacMillan (pb)

Charles Causley is another poet who spent years teaching younger children. His poems are characterized by their warmth, particularly towards the young, and also by their use of traditional forms such as the ballad. In no way a modernist, he is happy to write poems split up into regular verses, always following strong metres and a regular rhyming pattern. His fascination with history, and especially with the folklore of his native Cornwall, means that his subject matter often looks towards the past. The moving poem "Tavistock Goose Fair", for instance, describes his last memory of his father and "the feel of his iron hand on mine" before he went off to be killed in World War I when the poet was only four years old. Another poem describes some of the ups and downs of family life: "I wish I liked Aunt

Leonora/ When she draws in her breath like a hiss/ And
with fingers of ice and a grip like a vice/ She gives me a
walloping kiss." But whatever Causley writes, his superb
ear for words and sharp feeling for good – often slightly
sinister – stories mark him out as a born poet. His
*Selected Poems for Children*, chosen by him in his
eightieth year, comes with excellent illustrations by
John Lawrence.

## What is the Truth?
**Ted Hughes** (author) **Lisa Flather** (illustrator)
Faber (pb)

This collection, first
published in 1984, is an
extraordinary book. It
starts with a prose
conversation between
God and his son who
wants to visit earth and
discover the truth. God
warns him against trying
this, but his son is curious to
find out what it is really like
down there. By way of reply, God
asks various sleeping country
people to describe in their dreams the

truth about the animals they know best from their daily lives. These descriptions make up all the poems in this book, with the conversations throughout between God, his son and whoever they happen to be talking to taking place in prose. Finally God reveals that all these animals are in fact different forms of himself, but by this time his son is on earth and on his own, with the first cock just starting to crow.

Despite the presence of God and his Son, this is not a specifically Christian series of poems. Hughes wants instead to communicate the essence of each animal as directly as possible. He describes the hare, fox, cow, weasel, hedgehog and other animals exactly as they have always seemed to him with absolutely no sentimentality. The result is a mixture of earthy realism mixed with poetic fantasy. In "The Fly", Hughes launches straight into the kind of descriptiveness children immediately recognize and respond to: "In his black boiler suit, with his gas-mask, /His oxygen pack / His crampons, / He can get anywhere, explore any wreckage."

Hughes never flinches from discussing the nastier aspects of animal life, such as maggots, manure and casual murder. But there are other moments, such as the birth of a foal or the sight of a first swallow, when the poet registers his own wonder at the world of nature. He can also be very funny, as in his descriptions of "The Rat the Rat the Ratatat / The house poltergeist, shaped like a shuttle"; or else the sheep who "Is a machine / Of problems / For turning the Shepherd grey as a sheep". The energy of his metaphors and the vividness of his imagery makes this collection endlessly interesting and never predictable. Illustrated with simple but telling line drawings by Lisa Flather, this is a book that contains some of the most exciting modern verse ever written specifically for children.

9 to 11

# Index

# C

# D

# E

# F

# J

# K

# L

# M

# N

# O

# P

# R

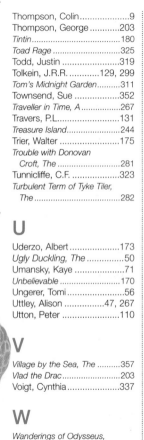

# U

# V

# W